Indian Ernie

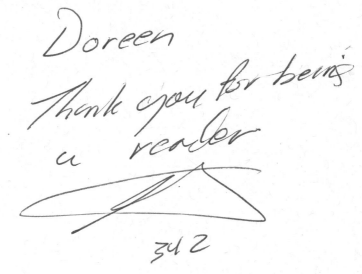

Doreen

Thank you for being

a reader

3u 2

Indian Ernie

PERSPECTIVES ON POLICING AND LEADERSHIP

by Ernie Louttit

Purich Publishing Ltd.
Saskatoon, Saskatchewan
Canada

Purich Publishing Ltd.
Box 23032, Market Mall Post Office
Saskatoon, SK Canada S7J 5H3
Phone: (306) 373-5311   Fax (306) 373-5315
E-mail: purich@sasktel.net
Website: www.purichpublishing.com

Library and Archives Canada Cataloguing in Publication

Louttit, Ernie, 1961–, author
    Indian Ernie : perspectives on policing and leadership / by Ernie Louttit.

ISBN 978-1-895830-78-1 (pbk.)

    1. Louttit, Ernie, 1961–. 2. Police—Saskatchewan—Saskatoon—Biography. 3. Native peoples—Saskatchewan—Saskatoon—Biography. 4. Marginality, Social—Saskatchewan—Saskatoon. 5. Saskatoon (Sask.)—Social conditions. I. Title.

HV7911.L69A3 2013   363.2092   C2013-907516-X

Editing, design and layout by Roberta Mitchell Coulter.
Cover design by Jamie Olson.
Cover photographs courtesy of the Saskatoon StarPhoenix.
Additional editorial assistance by Ursula Acton and Pamela Davison.
Printed and bound in Canada by Houghton Boston Printers and Lithographers, Saskatoon.
Purich Publishing Ltd. gratefully acknowledges the assistance of the Government of Canada through the Canada Book Fund, and the Creative Industry Growth and Sustainability Program made possible through funding provided to the Saskatchewan Arts Board by the Government of Saskatchewan through the Ministry of Parks, Culture and Sport for its publishing program.

Printed on 100% post-consumer, recycled, ancient-forest-friendly paper.

Canadian Patrimoine
Heritage canadien

Government
of
Saskatchewan
Ministry of Parks, Culture and Sport

SASKATCHEWAN
ARTS BOARD

This book is dedicated to my families:

*To my mother, Buzzy; my fathers, Jack and William;
my brothers, Shawn and Glen; and my sisters,
Tammy and Sherry (now deceased)*

*To my wife, Christine; sons Garret and Glen;
and daughters Gabrielle and Genna .*

To my brothers—too many to name—in the Canadian Forces

*To my brothers and sisters in the Police Services of Saskatchewan
and Canada: the many leaders—good and bad—who taught me
to lead, and those brave and noble people who help others for all
the right reasons, putting others ahead of themselves, knowing
their deeds would be known only to a few*

*Finally, to Don Purich and Karen Bolstad of Purich Publishing, my
editor Roberta Mitchell Coulter, and all of the editorial staff and
behind-the-scenes people for giving me the opportunity to tell
some of the many stories life has given me*

Contents

Preface   9

1.   Shoot or Don't Shoot   13

2.   Do You Know Your Dad's an Indian?   19

3.   Rough Start—Mine   25

4.   Rougher Starts—Theirs   35

5.   A Sense of Belonging   45

6.   No Ammunition Is Ever Surplus   53

7.   Leadership, Ego, and Arrogance   59

8.   Cheap and Destructive Highs   67

9.   One Strong Woman   77

10.   *Semper vigilans*—Assume Nothing   85

11.   Sticking My Nose In   93

12.   To Tell the Truth   99

13.   Murders and Major Crimes   103

14.   Dangerous Pursuits   117

15.   Training Ground   123

16.   Young Man Frozen   129

17.   Late Nights on the Streets   147

18. "We Know"—Who Knew?   153

19. Thinking on Your Feet   163

20. Cold Saves   167

21. A Family's Shame   171

22. The Truest of Warrior Spirits   177

23. 24/7—The Regular Stuff   183

Preface

I have always wanted to be brave and to move without fear and doubt. Brave not only in deeds, but in spirit and belief.

I was sitting on my back deck in late August of 2012, listening to an oldies radio station from Melfort, Saskatchewan. I was enjoying the warm sun and reminiscing. I was in my twenty-sixth year with the Saskatoon Police Service, and my friends were beginning to retire with alarming regularity. I could not help but wonder if it was not my time to retire as well.

Part of the leadership style I adopted years ago was to relate my experiences—good and bad—to younger officers so that they would not have to learn things the hard way like I did. As well, I found myself constantly explaining the police to native people and civilians in general, and explaining native people to the police. All in all, it was a lot of talking. Often when I was telling the stories, I would pick up extra people as an unintended audience and then get told, "Sarge, you should write a book."

I love to read, and I have always wanted to write, but for the longest time I did not think I was good enough to do justice to the written word I love so much. I had a short story published in 1991 in an anthology of native writers called *Voices*, and once I started writing, I could not stop. I filled notebook after notebook with my handwritten stories, and before I knew it, I had over a hundred pages and summer was coming to an end. The days were getting shorter, and it began to cool down. I began to doubt myself again, wondering if my stories would interest anyone or if my lack of education would take away from the content.

As I was writing, I began to realize the level of commitment it took to write. It was the same level of commitment the organizations I have worked with sometimes lacked, and lacked for probably the same reasons: fear of failure, lack of knowledge, and just being comfortable with the status quo can stop any organization from moving forward and trying new things. This is especially true of governmental organizations like the army and the police. The private sector will cut, slash, and expand as required. Governmental organizations will, if allowed, do just enough to get by.

It was not until I was in my forties that I could effectively articulate what I had known instinctively in my twenties: Everything is about commitment. If you are committed and passionate about what you do, you will be successful. I have an expression I used for years to explain my feelings about commitment: have your shit packed tight. It means have all of the things you need with you and ready so that, if you are called upon to do your job, you are physically and mentally prepared for any challenge. My tolerance for people who need to prepare for what they should have already been prepared for is very low. It is not too much to ask someone you work with to be ready to work.

When I graduated from the Saskatchewan Police College in 1987, I was the third native officer hired since the creation of the Saskatoon Police Service in 1903. I came to a department that seemed to have forgotten the people it was there to serve. Not all the officers, but certainly some of the senior officers had grown complacent and too comfortable with the way they did the business of policing. I felt there were some who believed the positions they occupied allowed them some moral and legal flexibility in how they got the job done.

I was too new and excited at first to realize what I was seeing, but soon I began to question why we did things the way we did. I began to question why we could not change things. I think this was happening in all police forces in North America at the time—progressive officers were questioning the status quo and realizing we were fast approaching an era where change was inevitable.

I in no way mean to dishonour the many dedicated police officers who served their careers with honour and purpose and risked their well-being for the citizens of our city. Some may, however, feel a sting. That cannot be helped. There will always be individual officers who are just incapable of change, for whatever reason. Those officers I believe are in the minority.

I think the young constables I started with in the late 1980s have for the most part learned how to lead and how to change. A better-educated and affluent society was beginning to demand more of the police and was holding them to a higher standard. Judges and lawyers were not accepting "This is the way we've always done it" as acceptable practice.

Most of my peers have either surpassed me in rank or retired. I stayed where I had chosen to be: out on the street and in the front lines. I wanted to ensure that I retired before I started resisting positive change. I have often been asked, if you were to leave a legacy, what would your legacy be? I hope our organization continues to be flexible and transparent, and that young constables will feel empowered to question questionable practices and leadership. A lot of the stories I have written about would not have happened if we had operated with the same transparency the Saskatoon Police Service operates with now.

When I started to write this, I worried it would not be relevant, but the more I thought about it, the more I was convinced that the lessons I had learned about stagnate thinking and inflexibility in policing were relevant.

1.

Shoot or Don't Shoot

It was almost seven o'clock and getting close to the end of the day shift when a call came in to our dispatch of an assault in progress. I was starting my third year with the Saskatoon Police Service. I knew the address and told the dispatcher that I was en route. I was not far off, and I pulled up in front of the apartment building within a minute. I did not wait for backup because the dispatcher's tone had implied that it was serious. I went to the east security door and used my knife to cheat the lock.

As soon as I entered the apartment building, I could hear screams and the sounds of a struggle from an apartment at the west end of the second floor. The building was decrepit, and the carpet crunched under my feet. I started to move toward the apartment, when a second officer arrived and pounded on the security door to be let in.

Together, we went to the apartment door. We listened for a couple of seconds. I could hear screaming and thuds, then a male voice saying, "Okay, enough. She's had enough."

My heart was racing. I steeled myself for whatever was behind the door. I tried the doorknob. It was not locked. It was blocked by a male, who immediately ran into a back bedroom. There was a smear of blood the width of a body from the kitchen toward a bedroom, like someone had dragged a wide, wet, bloody mop from one room to the other. A little boy about five years old looked at me with eyes as wide as saucers and said, "He killed my mom."

We pushed into the apartment, and as I glanced to my right, I saw several people in the living room. We followed the blood trail into the bedroom. The male who had run into the bedroom when we first entered the apartment was using his body to block the door so we could not get in. The other constable and I pushed the door open and flung the male blocking the door out into the hallway. In the bedroom, there was a crib containing a screaming infant and a mattress on the floor without a bed frame. I tried to turn on the light when we pushed our way into the room. It didn't work.

A man had straddled a woman on a mattress and was trying to shove a knife into her throat. She was holding the blade of the knife with her bare hands, trying to stop him from killing her. I recognized them both from previous calls. I pulled my revolver and yelled for him to drop the knife. He turned and looked at me, a crazed bloodlust in his eyes, and yelled, "Fuck you!"

He had no shirt on and was covered in blood. He had a tattoo of an eagle on his chest. I made that my aim point and kept yelling for him to drop the knife. He did not, and I started to pull the trigger. Slowly, the hammer came back—we were still using .38 calibre revolvers back then.

Time lost all meaning. What probably took milliseconds seemed like forever in the intensity of the moment. I was waiting for the explosion of the round discharging when he tossed the knife to his side.

I felt more than saw a big man coming up behind me. He reached and grabbed for my gun hand. He yelled, "You can't shoot my brother!" He yelled at me to shoot him instead. The fight was on. I pulled my gun close to my chest to protect it and started punching him. The second constable regained control and pushed the man out of the room again.

I could hear sirens and the thumping of boots in the hallway. It sounded like a stampede. The male who had tossed the knife was on his hands and knees trying to find it again. The woman was gurgling. The baby was still crying, and I did not know if the woman on the mattress was alive or dead.

There was another constable in the apartment by then, and the male who had told me to shoot him was being taken into custody. The male who had been stabbing the woman on the mattress gave up looking for the knife and charged as I was holstering my gun. Another officer hit him with a baton, slowing him down. I met his charge and flung him to the side. He went through the drywall and landed in the bathroom. I started hitting him, but another police officer—I think it was a patrol sergeant—pulled me off. Someone handcuffed the male.

I was covered in blood and was still in fight mode. I went to check on the woman. She had been severely beaten and was barely conscious. I called for an ambulance. I was stunned by all that had happened in sixty to ninety seconds.

Paramedics arrived and took her out and off to the hospital. One of the suspect's relatives, a woman, was told to take the children into the living room. The child in the crib was a ten-month-old girl. I picked her up and turned her over to the relative. I made a request for Identification section to come in to photograph the scene. I seized a club about seventy-five centimetres long that was covered in blood and a knife with a serrated, twenty-centimetre blade, also covered in blood. For some reason, no one took any statements. Everybody was cleared of the apartment and the children were turned over to a neighbour who was good friends with the victim. I locked up the apartment after Identification section was finished processing the scene.

I went to the hospital to check on the victim's condition. The doctor who was treating her told me that she had extensive bruising to the face, shoulders, both arms, and her chest. The cuts on her fingers took fifteen stitches to close. The doctor said she was weak but she could talk.

I went into the trauma room and asked her what had happened. She told me her husband had done this to her because her aunt had come over to see the children.

It was obvious that she needed rest, and I did not question her any further. I told her I would come to her home as soon as she was released from hospital.

I went to the station to read both the males their charges. After I told the husband his charges, he said, "Holy fuck! Tell her I love her."

I then went to sit down in the detention area to make my notes. I was shaking with adrenaline and still covered in blood. Other officers came and went. They looked at me but said nothing. I guess I was there for about an hour when the corporal suggested I should go clean up and leave my report.

I showered and changed. It was the changeover between day shift and night shift, and all the constables were meeting at a local cop bar. My girlfriend, now my wife, was coming there to meet me after she was done work. I got there and ordered a beer. Some of the guys asked me what had happened. I don't remember if I told them or not. My girlfriend got there, and I guess I just sat there sort of shell-shocked until she finally said, "If you're not talking, I am going to leave," so I shook it off. Sometimes talking about things can just wreck the night.

The next night, I went to the victim's apartment and got a written statement. Her hands were too badly injured to write, so she dictated it to me. She told me her aunt had come over to visit the children. Her husband went to the bedroom because he was mad. He began to yell at her to come to the bedroom. When she said no, he got up and came into the kitchen. She asked him why he was so upset just because her aunt was there. He stood up to strike her. She broke a beer bottle and told him to stay away from her. He hit her with something, in all likelihood the club. He hit her repeatedly, and she tried to escape the apartment. He grabbed a knife in the kitchen, grabbed her by the hair, and began to pull her back into the apartment. He tried to stab her in the throat. She blocked the knife with her fingers. He told her he was going to kill her this time. She pleaded with him not to. Another male tried to stop the husband, but he was pushed aside. She managed to get into the hallway but was dragged back into the apartment.

She could not remember much after that. She knew she was dragged into the bedroom. He was hitting her with the club, kicking, punching, and choking her. When she came to, she saw a knife coming right for her throat again.

So many things happened to her she could not remember all of it.

She turned over the bloody sheets and clothing to me, and I told her to call me if anybody threatened her or tried to dissuade her from testifying. I made arrangements for her to stay at a women's shelter and left her.

Months later, the matter went to a preliminary hearing. I had modified the charges after I had gotten her statement. He was charged with attempted murder, unlawful confinement, threats to cause death, and assaulting police.

The wife had by now become a reluctant witness. She testified, and then I was up. Because of the seriousness of the charges, the head lawyer at Saskatoon Legal Aid had taken the defendant's case. She was very aggressive, and I spent hours on the stand. She asked point-blank if I would have shot her client and was outraged when I told her I was in the process of doing that when he saved his own life by tossing the knife away. She asked who was in charge of the investigation. She asked why no other statements were taken other than the one the wife provided. I didn't really have a good answer for her.

The husband was committed for trial at the Court of Queen's Bench and remained in custody.

No detectives were ever assigned to assist me, and no detectives offered to help or to provide me with advice. No one from the administration asked if I was all right. I knew I had a long road ahead of me with the Saskatoon Police Service.

This incident was my first real down-to-the-wire, shoot-or-don't-shoot test. I could have shot him, but I didn't, and at the end of it all, I'm glad I didn't. I knew I would have if he hadn't dropped the knife. I knew and accepted that at some time in my career I might have to shoot someone. I was not playing police anymore. I was there.

Months later, a trial date was set. The wife was nowhere to be found. The charges were stayed.

The wife did not resurface until a couple of years later, when I tried to stop a drunk driver who threw the car she was driving into reverse and crashed it into my patrol car. She was the drunk driver.

The husband remained an active criminal. We caught him after a high-speed chase from a break-and-enter where thousands of dollars' worth of cigarettes had been stolen. He and an accomplice were pursued from the scene in a stolen truck. They were chased into a farmer's field, and the wheat stubble caused the truck to catch fire and burn, along with all the stolen cigarettes.

The wife apparently overdosed in Regina shortly afterward. The husband still lives in Saskatoon.

My mother, older brother (left), me, and my younger brother (front) at church somewhere in southern Ontario (courtesy the author)

2.

Do You Know Your Dad's an Indian?

One summer I took my son to Northern Ontario to visit my family. He was not quite four years old. We were up visiting my father at his trailer on top of a hill. He had converted the trailer into a small summer home. We were outside having coffee when my son whispered to me, "Dad, I need to talk to you." I thought maybe he had to go to the bathroom and was shy because it was an outhouse. He was very insistent, so I went around the corner of the trailer with him. I asked what the problem was. With all the solemnity and sincerity a child can have, my son looked me in the eye and asked, "Dad, do you know your dad's an Indian?"

My name is Ernie Louttit. People on the street call me Indian Ernie. I suppose it makes sense. I am a Cree Indian and my name is Ernie.

I have been police officer for thirty years. Twenty-seven of those years have been with the Saskatoon Police Service.

Like so many native people, I've struggled with my identity. Because I came from an isolated community and was raised without the influence of television and daily papers, I somehow formed my own opinion about what I thought a "Good Indian" was. I went out of my way to show I could work, and to show I could take whatever anyone threw my way. I don't know if it was because of Canadian society's conditioning of native people, or the native tradition of understating our successes, but somehow I always had the feeling that it was not quite good enough.

Traditionally, most native people disliked or discouraged anyone from being too loud, boisterous, or confrontational. I found over the years that most elders were uncomfortable with me. Too brash and impatient and not willing to embrace traditional teaching, I was never quite sure where my place was.

Even while I was policing, the identity struggle continued. I stayed on the street my whole career because I wanted to be there, mostly for the native community. Because of where I worked, the majority of people I had arrested were native. While policing, I was called an apple, a white man's Indian, and a token Indian. I've even had numerous death threats over the years.

After a while, everybody had a story about Indian Ernie. Sometimes I would arrest someone who didn't know me who would tell me stories about Indian Ernie. Ironically, while trying to be treated like everyone else, I had established, for better or worse, my own identity: Indian Ernie.

From the start of my career, I had to wear three hats. I was a policeman, a native man, and—at first reluctantly—a leader. As a native man, I wanted to be seen as capable and equal to anyone. I never needed a hand up, I just needed no one standing in my way. I could see the need for leadership in the communities I worked with, but at the start of my police career I was like the kid in the back of the crowd hoping no one would pick me.

When I started policing, the federal government and some segments of Canadian society still had a paternalistic attitude toward natives, and the police were not immune to it. In the cities, especially in western Canada, the smoldering issues of racism—on both sides—and the ability of different groups to be tolerant of each other would be tested. I've often said to people that in my opinion, native people want the same things in regard to justice as everyone else: They want to be free of the criminals. They don't want to walk in fear of anyone, including the police.

This is where the line gets blurry for me. I know the circumstances and background of native offenders, and in spite of my knowledge, I know they still have to be held to account for their criminal acts. I believe in justice first and forgiveness second. I believe in personal accountability before communal acceptance of responsibility.

Policing has changed so much since the first time I pinned on a badge and strapped on a gun belt. I am starting to feel left behind. Not in a sad or melancholy way, but rather with a sense of pride. I am the new old-school breed of police.

The old-school police I challenged and fought with through most of my career have long since passed into stories and lessons for those police officers either longing for the good old days or never wanting to repeat them. My service with the Saskatoon Police Service had its share of confrontations and controversies, but those incidents did not define it. I love the Saskatoon Police Service and marvel at how far it has progressed. I love the young men and women who are its soul and admire the courage and bravery of most of them. Still, for any of the hard-learned lessons to be effective, they need to be told and retold.

When I started with the Saskatoon Police, the old boys' club was in charge. The senior investigators in the Saskatoon Police Department when I started were veteran police officers. They learned their techniques as they went. There was not a lot of formal training. They were used to getting their own way and were not used to being challenged in any way, shape, or form. They did not like to be questioned and were never second-guessed. The administration was one or two generations older than these detectives and even more inflexible and rigid. There were good detectives, I just hardly ever dealt with them. They worked away quietly, solving crimes and working within the established hierarchy and system.

I know my experiences have been repeated in various forms by other officers in other departments, and hopefully the end result will be fair and more transparent police services for all Canadians.

The first love any police officer should have, besides family, is for the community he or she serves. If you do not love your community, all the negative things you see and deal with will cause you to be bitter and cynical. Them-versus-us is a familiar and sad old story that almost always ends badly.

Police have to remember always Peel's rule. Peel said the police are the people and the people are the police. Never think that you are more important or better than the people you deal with. If you do, you become the old stereotyped brute-force police officer so often portrayed in the media: unresponsive and uncaring, bound by convention, and out of touch with the realities of the community.

Saskatoon, Regina, Winnipeg, and most major western Canadian cities have high native populations. They also have very high crime rates. Most of the crime is, of course, linked to income. When I first started with the Saskatoon Police, the majority of native people living in the city had the lowest incomes. Remove the term "native," however, and they were just poor people.

When you're a police officer, it's easy to treat poor people poorly. They do not complain very often. They are stoic in their struggles. They have been conditioned to a hard life. They accept things most people wouldn't, and they forgive things most people consider unforgivable.

Here's where the best tool a police officer has on his web belt comes in, and here is where most dangerous things occur if the police officer does not have it. The tool is empathy. To me, the ability to put yourself in someone else's place is what defines a police officer.

When it comes to finding their empathy tank, there are a lot of things going against someone who has been raised well, is educated, and has lived without conflict. Sincerity cannot be faked. It's one of the most transparent of human emotions. Lack it and you lack credibility.

I love the people of Saskatoon—the good people, the bad people, the lost, and even the self-righteous—because they taught me every day. Every day I learned a lesson in life, of unbounded generosity and kindness, unspeakable cruelty and depravity, how to cope, and how to live.

I've been in the same area of Saskatoon for almost my whole career. It has many names: alphabet city, Harlem of the prairies, and the hood. The population was primarily native, and when I started they were poor and crime-ridden.

The neighbourhood has changed over the years. The crime rate is still high, but there is progress all around. There are new housing projects, new schools, and more employment. Progress is starting to choke out the crime.

Throughout my career, there has been a core of people who always, in spite of all the obstacles, moved steadily forward, the people from social agencies, friendship centres, and families who refused to knuckle down. These people shielded the children and protected them from everything they could. When they lost them to street gangs or drugs or crime, the mothers and fathers, grandmothers and grandfathers stood by them while they did the time and accepted them back without judgment or questions.

I would like to be able to say it doesn't matter what race you are, people will see you for who you are. But that is not the way life is. My being native mattered to a lot of people. It affected the way they treated me. It affected the way they saw me and judged me. No person is ever free of prejudice, but how a person manifests their prejudices is the test of their morality.

There are so many things people will not talk about. Sometimes not talking about things that trouble us, like our prejudices, is as damaging as our prejudices themselves.

If you are an Indian in Canada, everything now is about the choices you make and the paths you choose to walk on. There is still prejudice, and a lot of communities are still struggling. But as an individual, you will make the choices that will affect you for the rest of your life.

First off, you need to be proud of the fact you are native. Not in a boisterous, in-your-face way, but rather in the quiet, dignified way of our forefathers and the elders. Telling people how proud you are to be a native sometimes means you are not really that proud at all. Pride is a visible strength which shows in how you conduct and carry yourself. You can be the poorest person and still have pride.

The second and equally important thing you need to remember is to expect nothing from anyone for nothing. You need to earn a living and support your family. You need to work. If you take the view that our treaty rights will support you, you are wrong.

Third, never let the people who hate bring you down to their level. Outlast them by achievement. Being native in Canada now means opportunity. If you stay in school and steer clear of crime and gangs, there are unlimited opportunities for you. Corporations, governments, police, and other groups actively plan strategies directly linked to getting natives into their work force.

I have never been a traditional Indian. My analogy is, I am like a warrior who sleeps outside the camp: No one really wants to see or hear from you until you are needed. I know a lot of people draw strength from tradition, and it is important to maintain some traditions. At the same time, we need to create new traditions and adapt to change. There will always be some people in any group those who get left behind, and that cannot be helped. We all need to push forward for the future generations.

I like to think that I have pushed forward, although I was always reluctant to think that I could be seen as a role model. All of us have our own faults and character flaws. I have always tried to be as honest as I could about how I felt. Age and maturity help to embolden the way we talk as our beliefs and convictions are entrenched with time. The way I dealt with racists and prejudice was by example. I would work and let the results from my work speak for me. I would outlast people who put obstacles in front of me.

I am a native and am proud of being a police officer. Sometimes I wish I were seen as police officer who just happens to be native. But as I said, sometimes my being native was very important to some people.

I have now retired, and I hope accomplished my goals: training my replacements, and giving people a different view of the police and who they are. I hope I inspired some native kids to see policing as a true and honourable profession that they want to be part of.

It took me years to learn how to deal with people, but I believe the insight people gave me is transferable. If I can give anyone insight without the sting of hard-learned lessons, I will.

3.

Rough Start—Mine

My parents divorced when I was young. My early years were spent in a small town in northern Ontario called Oba. My mother, with my older brother and me, left Oba after the collapse of her marriage. She went to several small towns in Northern Ontario, working at various jobs to support us. She met and fell in love with a roguish, good-looking man, who took her and her two sons into his life. When he was sober, he was a charming, hard-working man. When he was drunk, he was a steel-fisted wife beater.

My mother had two children with him. My little sister and brother were blue-eyed and beautiful. They and my older brother, who was fair-skinned with auburn hair, were explainable. And then there was me. Brown and dark, there was never any question I was not his.

I'm sure he would have found other reasons to beat my mother, but I was convenient. He would drink his whiskey and go from laughing to dark as predictably as the coming of a violent summer storm. My mother tried to placate him. It never worked. We would run and hide. My mother would absorb the punches.

Our neighbours knew and occasionally would call the police when it got too bad. The police would come and defer to him. They would suggest he come down to the drunk tank to cool down. Never mind my mother's bloodied face and black eyes. They never attempted to handcuff him. He was a very tough man.

There was an elderly woman who ran a small corner store across from the hotel behind our house. My mother would send me there to keep her company on the weekends. I don't know if my absence lessened the violence my mother endured. I was too young to understand my mother's reasoning.

It was in southern Ontario where I had my first conscious encounters with racism. My stepfather had made me aware that I was different from other kids. There were not a lot of native kids in Thorold, Ontario. My stepfather regularly referred to me as the little black bastard. At school I would be taunted with the chants of "Where's your bow, Geronimo?" Kids would regularly do war whoops and dance around in the style of Hollywood Indians. The worst part was that a lot of the kids were older, bigger, and stronger than me. They should have known better, but they had to have learned those attitudes somewhere.

All the same, even when I got beat up at school, it didn't come close to the intensity of what was happening in our home. So you just endured.

In an offbeat way, I thank these people for making me who I am today. My stepfather's cruelty and the mean-spirited treatment of the other kids thickened my skin. As difficult as this was, I think all of this started me off on the road to becoming a police officer. I was frustrated by the injustice of it all.

When my mother finally had enough, we ran. My mother, God bless her, had scrimped and saved until we had enough money to take a train back to Oba, where we had started from. We got to Oba with the clothes on our backs and no money to speak of. My aunt helped us to get settled. Being so young, I had no idea of all the things my mother was going through.

Oba, our new refuge and new home, was and still is a unique place. Isolated and over sixty kilometres from any other town, it had its own very distinctive character. When we first arrived back there, the town had a general store, two hotels, a railway station, and a one-room school. The businesses were the only ones to have electricity, which was supplied by diesel generators. There were only a few phones in town. There was no road connecting us with anywhere else. Everything came in by rail. The reason Oba was there was because the Algoma Central Railway crossed the Canadian National Railway at that point, and their junction created a large railway yard for the transfer of loads of wood and iron ore.

The village had a population of about 120 people, and every one of them was a character. My mother used to say that if there was an eccentric nonconformist who did not fit anywhere else in society, they would end up in Oba. There were trappers, railway workers, lumberjacks, and miscellaneous entrepreneurs and business owners populating the town. Even with two hotels, there were bootleggers, and drinking was an accepted pastime.

When we first got off the train, my mother, with my little brother and sister in tow, went to her sister's. My brother and I got into a rock fight with the local boys.

Oba was a great place to be after our trials and tribulations in southern Ontario. Hunting, fishing, and guns were all an accepted part of the culture there. Unfortunately, almost everyone's parents had issues, and alcohol was a part of everyday life.

My older brother was readily accepted. My younger brother just didn't care, and my little sister was too young to know the difference. I was couple of years younger than everyone else and a bit overweight. I was a convenient target and bore the brunt of a lot of kids' frustrations. I fought and lost a lot.

Even in this little town, there was racism, and people had no reservations about expressing their opinions on different races. The politically correct atmosphere of today did not exist back then. The lines in this place were pretty clearly drawn. Being white and English was good, and being white and French was okay. Italians, Germans, Ukrainians and any other Eastern Europeans were DPs, an old-fashioned term for displaced persons from World War II—good, hard-working people who were never quite good enough for everyone else. Lastly, there were Indians, predetermined to be drunk and lazy. Unfortunately, some native people acted in a manner reinforcing the prevailing stereotypes, drinking until they passed out wherever the drink had taken them and lying there visible to everyone. They would get paid, get drunk, and miss work.

We initially stayed in a room at my auntie's hotel until my mother met a young Frenchman who eventually became our stepfather. He was twelve years younger than my mother. He totally committed himself to her, and by proxy to us. He turned out to be a very good man and is still with my mother forty years on. He was a good father to my younger brother and sister and the first to accept my younger brother when he announced he was gay. My older brother and I were just too cynical, but just accepted the status quo. I wanted nothing to do with him, but ever the faithful son, I accepted him begrudgingly.

We moved into a small two-bedroom home that had once been a bunkhouse for the Lands and Forests detachment. It was heated by an oil stove and a wood-burning stove. We didn't have electricity or running water. The boys used the outhouse out back. My sister got a chamber pot. We hauled water in buckets from the tap in the baggage room of the railway station. We used coal oil lamps for lighting.

I would not trade those years for anything. Before we got electricity and a phone, we spent many hours together in the kitchen sharing the heat and light, and it brought us closer together than we were when we had modern conveniences. Still, it was not all peace and tranquility—there were drinking parties, fights, and drama once again, but without the intensity and violence of southern Ontario.

I learned to read in our one-room school, and I became and still am a voracious reader. Reading took me places I could not realistically go to anytime soon. I would pretend I was Tecumseh, General Brock, or one of the other half-dozen heroes I admired. My heroes were almost always underdogs, doomed to fight outnumbered and against great adversity.

The teachers who taught at Oba Public School were mixed bag of characters, even more diverse than the townspeople. The first teacher I remember was a tall, skinny, grey-haired Englishman who was even more old-fashioned than our old-fashioned school. He was strict and played favourites based on the social status of the students in our little town. He also drank while he was teaching and occasionally was too drunk to finish the day's lessons. He would drunkenly ring the handheld bell to summon us back to class at lunch or recess. If his speech was too slurred, we just did not come back.

The next teacher after him was a short, bisexual man from southern Ontario. He was a dynamic and inspiring teacher. He did his best to let us see the possibilities before us when we would eventually leave this little school. He got the first videocassette recorder we had ever seen and let us watch the moon landing. He had us make a map of the world which covered the entire wall of the school. He even offered to adopt me so I could get the post-secondary education he knew my mother could not provide. Unfortunately, he also drank too much. During one drinking episode, he fell into the snow on the way home from the hotel and suffered frostbite to his hands. We missed several days of school while he healed.

My last teacher in Oba was a woman. She had graduated at the top of her teaching class in Ontario and she came down to Oba to teach us with all the zeal of the newly graduated. We had been fairly loosely taught. Although we had been given the important lessons in math and reading, we were used to making allowances for the eccentric behaviour of our teachers and were not really full-time students. We were used to the freedom to hunt and fish whenever we felt like it. As a consequence, I found myself kicked out of school a couple of times before I finished grade eight.

Oba is still there, although the station, school, the two hotels, and the store are gone. There has been a road to Oba for about thirty years now, a strip of gravel cut through the woods to link up with the rest of the world. There are only eight people living there permanently. Most of the houses and bunkhouses are now, for all intents and purposes, cabins or camps for former residents who come back whenever they can to try to recapture the way Oba was back in the seventies. It will always be a special place for me. A melting pot of cultures and technologies, Oba taught me about the diversity of people and how it was not my place to judge people because of the paths they had chosen. I go back at least twice a year to hunt and fish. It is where I wash my soul. Everyone needs an Oba.

At the end of grade eight, my brother and I, having graduated at the same time, had to go to a town north of Oba called Hearst to attend high school. We had to take the train every Sunday night and stay there until the train returned Saturday morning. Elementary school had had some challenges, but you could always go home at the end of the day. In Hearst there was no going home.

We stayed in boarding houses. I quickly got the feeling that I was a pay cheque and nothing more. They were cold and unfriendly places. Poor meals and thin soup were the order of the day, and I always felt like an unwelcome intruder.

I got into a fight on the first day of school with some jock who made fun of the way the kids from Oba dressed. He was taunting the girls in the cafeteria, and I called him outside to fight. As we were fighting, the principal came out of his office, which was directly above the area where we were fighting, and grabbed me by the shoulder. In French, he asked the boy I was fighting with if he wanted the police to be called. Thankfully, and to his credit, the boy answered in English that he didn't need the police. He was the son of one of the prominent businessman in Hearst. He had broken his finger when he grazed a punch off my head. He was also a local hockey star. This incident told me a lot about how high school was going to go.

Still on my first day, I was assigned to my homeroom. It was called 14A. It was situated in a hallway between the two wings of the school, which formed an H. It was a room for all the native students, regardless of grade. The dropout rate among native students was high. The theory was that native students would support each other and therefore more native students would graduate.

My brother, who looks white, went to a homeroom for all grade nine English-speaking students. While I was in the office after the fight, I asked the principal why I was not with my brother. He looked surprised and asked who my brother was. When I told him my brother's name, he quickly looked up the file. He offered to put me with my brother, but my temper was up, and I told him he had made his point: my brother and I, from the same hometown and having the same last name, had been separated by my physical appearance only.

The separate homeroom had the exact opposite effect on the native students. They felt isolated and never really included in the mainstream of the school. Most of the people I started grade nine with in homeroom 14A never graduated.

There were other surprises in the following weeks. I had to show my money in one restaurant before they would serve me. The word "*sauvage*" now entered my vocabulary. I heard it time and time again when I went into a store and when I was walking in the hallways. The natives in the school were not very friendly either as I lived in town and not on the reserve. My brother tried to include me with his peers, but I never really felt welcome. I became raceless, never really fitting in with either group.

I drifted toward other marginalized students. Hanging out with the marginalized kids had its own set of perils, and I turned to smoking marijuana and drinking. I developed my love for heavy metal music around then, and it became kind of the soundtrack of my life for the next thirty years. Just a little angry and hinting at dangerous, it was a good thing for me. There were good teachers and good people who gently nudged me back on to the right path when it looked like I was going to spin out of control.

I dated French girls, but peer pressure and their parents usually made short work of those relationships. I dated native girls, but my brother told me it was looked down upon to date native girls. Their friends also applied peer pressure to ensure that those relationships did not go anywhere.

My French teacher told me point blank that he did not like people like me in his class and that I would pass his class if I did not attend. In classes where I was interested, like English, history, and shops, I did all right. The rest of classes left a lot to be desired.

I dropped out of high school in grade eleven.

When I was fifteen, I lied about my age and got hired onto a tie gang working in Northern Ontario. The tie gang was a labour gang, partially mechanized, that removed old or damaged railway ties and replaced them. We could replace up to a thousand railway ties in a single day. We had a cook car and slept in Atco trailers on flatcars. The food was good, and the work was honest.

I had hair down to the small of my back and was skinny, tall, and gangly. The foreman was a short, tough Portuguese man. A career railway man, he was notorious for his temper and for firing anybody who didn't work up to his standards. When I reported to him, he took one look at me and in his thickly accented English said, "You long-haired hippie *cockasucker*, you will be home with your mama in three days."

He gave me the worst job on the gang. In the winter, special trains would drop metal kegs full of railway spikes along the portion of the line where the ties were to be replaced. The kegs, which weighed twenty-five to thirty kilograms, would roll into the ditches along the right-of-way. My job was to go ahead of the gang and bring the kegs up the embankments, open them, and lay out four spikes per railway tie. Because the gang was mechanized, you had to work fast. Along with the heat and mosquitoes, it was backbreaking work, and back then I didn't weigh much more than sixty-five kilograms.

Most guys quit within a couple of days, but I began to take pride in the fact that I kept doing the job. About two weeks in, the foreman, who had not spoken a word to me since the first time, came up to me and said, "You long-haired hippie *cockasucker*, you awork ahard." He gave me a hammer used to spike railway spikes into the ties and asked me to spike a spike in. My first swing, I broke the hammer handle. The foreman gave me a disgusted look and sent me back to the front of the gang to bring the spikes back up to the tracks.

Even though we worked twelve- to fourteen-hour days, every night I would practise spiking spikes into ties. About a week later, I could drive a spike into a tie with three hits and never broke a hammer. Someone must have told the foreman because one morning as I was heading out to the front of the gang he stopped me and gave me a hammer. He sent me to the back of the gang, where I was a spiker for the rest of the summer until I had to return to school. The foul-tempered company man who very rarely smiled taught me what it meant to work. I've no idea what became of him or his tie gang, but I will always be grateful for the lesson he taught me.

The money and freedom I had on the railway were too enticing to allow me to settle into high school again. After I quit school, I got hired as a section man again with the CNR. I loved the work and the people I worked with. It was hard, honest work, and I have never been afraid of working. I bid on various jobs and worked sections all over Northern Ontario.

One of my foremen, an Ojibwa Indian, started telling me stories about being in the army, and he encouraged me to join.

I found myself in North Bay, Ontario, in the fall of 1978, on my way to see a band at a local bar. I was seventeen years old and had hair down to my waist, and no one ever asked me for identification. I had been going to bars for years by then. As I was walking on the main street, I could hear a song being piped onto the street. In retrospect, it was the cheesiest song ever. It went, "There is no life like it, and I won't forget the day, when I chose to live the Force's way." Deep baritone voices, they sounded like a barbershop quartet, but it got my attention. I stopped in front of the Canadian Forces Recruiting Centre.

There was a life-size cardboard picture of a soldier holding a rifle, wearing a helmet and web gear. He looked tough and professional. The hook was set. I went in and nervously told an immaculately uniformed soldier that I wanted to join. He looked me up and down and told me I had to write a test. The band was not on for a few hours, so I thought what the hell. He took me to a room and gave me the test. It seemed easy, and I was done in no time. The test seemed to be all common-sense stuff.

He took the test away, and I sat in the front office looking at the tanks, helicopters, and ships in the various pamphlets, waiting for him to come back. A few minutes later, he came out told me I could join any trade except pilot because I did not have the education. I had already decided I wanted to join the infantry. I did not want to be a tradesman. I wanted to be a soldier and told him so. He began to argue with me—the infantry would be a waste of my intelligence and skills. We were bantering back and forth when another soldier came out of a back office. He was an officer with the red-and-white shoulder flash of the Princess Patricia's Canadian Light Infantry, a renowned Canadian infantry regiment. His uniform was even more immaculate than the sergeant's.

He asked what the problem was, and I told him the sergeant would not let me join the infantry. The officer looked at the sergeant and told him he would take over from there. The officer took me to his office and congratulated me on my choice of trade. It was getting close to the end of the day, and the recruiting office would soon be closed, but it didn't seem to make a difference to him. Soon he was on the phone to a local doctor. The officer drove me to a big house where an ancient doctor led me to an examination room. The doctor made the officer wait outside in a sitting area. He asked if I liked girls and if I had any problems physically. I told him yes to the girls and no to the physical problems, and after an appropriate amount of time had passed the doctor came out and told the officer I was good to go.

The officer drove us back to the recruiting office and there I swore the oath of allegiance. I was in, almost. Because I was only seventeen, I had to get my mother's signature. It was getting late, but nonetheless the officer issued me travel orders and instructions to travel home, obtain the signature, and report back to North Bay prior to basic training.

That day I made what for me was a momentous and critical decision that changed my life for the better, and I have never regretted it. Any young man or woman—native or any other ethnic background—who is not quite sure where they want to go with their life could not go too far wrong by joining the Canadian Armed Forces.

I was not totally naïve to things military. I was an avid reader of military history. This, however, was the real thing, and I would soon find out what I was made of.

Trying to play the guitar at Oba, summer of 1978 (courtesy the author)

4.

Rougher Starts—Theirs

When I first started with the Saskatoon Police Department, the parenting crisis caused by the residential school system was going through its last painful throes, and the frequency of child apprehensions was shocking to me. The parents' addictions and lack of parenting skills left the children vulnerable to people wanting to exploit them. The area I worked in put me in the front lines of the difficult battle native people were fighting to right the wrongs of the past, and still, to this day, the legacy resonates.

One afternoon on a day shift, a call came in of a fire in an apartment building. I arrived and saw smoke billowing from a ground-floor apartment. As I entered the hallway, several people pointed to the apartment and told me that there were kids inside. Smoke was seeping under the door as I reached for the doorknob. The door was locked. I could hear someone crying. I kicked open the door and was immediately knocked back by the superheated air. I hit the wall on the opposite side of the hallway. I sank down to my knees and started to make a different plan. I knew better than to go into a fire standing up, but because there were children there, I had forgotten the most basic rule: get low so the smoke does not get you. Smoke from fires in modern structures almost always contains some sort of toxins because of the building materials we use. Acrid and bitter, it is the smoke, not the fire, that will make you a casualty.

I knew I was going to try to go in again. As I steeled myself to start crawling in, I looked up and saw two firefighters with air packs and masks coming down the hallway. The sounds of their breathing and voices were distorted by the masks. I was coughing and could barely talk as I relayed the information that there were at least two kids in the apartment. Like apparitions, they passed by me and entered the apartment.

I went to the entrance door of the apartment building as more fire-fighters started coming in. I gulped huge breaths of fresh air as the fire-fighters came out of the apartment with two children and two adults. Other occupants of the apartment came up to me and told me that the adults in the apartment had been drinking and doing drugs all day.

The firefighters began to deploy huge fans to clear the smoke from the building. One of firefighters told me that there had not been an ac-tual fire. An aluminum pot had been left on the stove and had boiled dry, creating superheated air and smoke. After the apartment was relatively clear of the white smoke, I went in and looked around.

The two-bedroom apartment was filthy. There were used syringes, capped and uncapped, in every room. In the bedroom where the children had been sleeping, I saw an electrical cord tied around the doorknob. The electrical cord had been used to tie the bedroom door shut so that the kids could not get out. In the bathroom, the doors of the vanity had been removed, and toilet cleaner and other chemicals were within easy reach of a crawling child. The bathtub was filled with over ten centimetres of water. There were many other hazards, but those were the most glaring when I did a quick walk-through.

I went back outside into the fresh air. My eyes were burning and my throat was sore. I could not imagine what it had been like in the bed-room for those kids.

The father seemed fine. I knew him from previous dealings. He was a drug addict and was mute. His common-law wife was a prostitute. She was in a fire truck with an oxygen mask on. I asked paramedics if the father was all right. When they said he was, I arrested him for child endangerment. The other occupants of the apartment building ap-plauded and made catcalls to the father as I was handcuffing him. Other officers arrived, and we quickly got the scene sorted out. As soon as the firefighters and paramedics released the mother, I arrested her as well. It seemed like a no-brainer. The children were not hurt. Social Services seized them.

Other officers transported the parents to the cells, and I stayed and took statements. The Identification section came and photographed the scene. I seized the electrical cord and other evidence. When I was done, I went in and left my report.

The local media ran with the story, and the parents—understand-ably—were portrayed as they should have been. The legal aid lawyer who was appointed to defend them, however, spoke to reporters and said the police (meaning me) were heavy-handed. She said that the parents had been unnecessarily vilified, and their addictions were a social problem and not a matter for the courts. Her office must have applied some pressure somewhere because shortly after this incident an order came out. We were not to lay charges of child endangerment or child neglect without the consent of the Crown Prosecutor's Office. The criminal charges against the parents were stayed; they were charged under *The Saskatchewan Child Protection Act* and received fines.

The mother still lives in Saskatoon. Where the father is and where the children ended up I have no idea.

At the end of it all, my hands did not feel heavy at all.

I got a call from an informant out of the blue. The informant did not want anything or need anything. He told me to check a house in the centre of the Riversdale neighbourhood. He didn't elaborate. I did not know what to think of the call. I knew which house he was talking about. It was a small rental house where I'd been many times. The renters changed as often as the seasons, and I did not know who was renting it when I received the call.

When I got out of my car, I could smell the house from the street. The front door was ajar, a couple of windows were broken, and their screens were torn and hanging. I went to the front door. The smell of feces and rotting meat was overpowering. I was gagging and about to step back when I saw a kid about eight years of age trying to hide behind a pile of garbage.

I stepped into the house and quickly found two more kids. They were wild-eyed and filthy. Their teeth were black. Their unwashed bodies were clad in filthy clothes. The oldest was eleven, and the other two were seven and eight years old. They were all malnourished. The water had been cut off and the toilet was overflowing. Not wanting to leave the house at night, the kids took to defecating in different rooms.

I was trying not to gag, and I didn't want to frighten these kids any worse than they were frightened already. I called for another car and requested Social Services to attend. I walked them outside, and we sat by my car until I got some help there.

We established that the mother had left the children to their own devices approximately three weeks earlier. They had been fending for themselves ever since—no school, no power, and no food. How they survived without coming to the attention of the police or Social Services was beyond me. How a situation like this could be allowed to happen in the city without somebody noticing bothers me to this day.

The children were apprehended by Social Services. I called the Identification section to come in to photograph the squalor and prepared a case against the mother. The stench was so bad that I told the corporal coming to photograph the scene to bring a mask. Flies and other bugs were everywhere.

I had no idea where the mother was. I left my report and requested a warrant for her arrest on three counts of child abandonment.

I was going on leave to Northern Ontario and was served a court notice just before I left. The mother had been arrested in northern Saskatchewan on the strength of my warrants. A short trial date has been set, and I was required to return early. It was long trip back and hard to leave after a short visit. I got back, found out she had changed her plea to guilty, and I was not required to testify.

I never knew her story and why she had abandoned her children. I don't know if she ever got her children back. Like so many things in my career, there are some things it is just better not to know.

There is a school in the centre of the Pleasant Hill community in Saskatoon. It's older, with the classic architecture of the early 1900s. It stands like a castle in the centre of what had become, when I was assigned there as a patrol officer, a very troubled community. In the late eighties and early nineties, I had lots of contact with the teachers and staff of the school. The staff, a dedicated team of teachers and administrators, worked tirelessly to protect their charges. Most of the children lived in poverty and were surrounded by crime. Many of them went to school hungry. Most of the children who attended the school were native.

At one time, there were four convicted pedophiles living in apartments within a block of the school. To the north, south, east, and west, the school was surrounded. I got a call from one of the teachers, who told me that a young girl—I'll call her Rose for the purposes of this story—had been coming to school with new clothes and money. She was now very popular. She was a freckle-faced native girl, skinny, awkward, and vulnerable. The teacher was concerned because other young girls were flocking to her with her newfound affluence.

Normally, you would just be happy when a poor kid catches a break. In this case, in an area rife with prostitution and drug dealing, prosperity is a warning flag.

Rose lived with her grandmother as her mother was trapped in a cycle of prostitution and drugs. I went to see her grandmother and asked if I could talk to Rose. The grandmother appeared shocked that I was there—*Kokum* told me she did not think the police would care—and she was very forthcoming. Rose, she told me, had taken to disappearing for long periods of time on the weekends. Rose had been defensive and argumentative when *Kokum* questioned her about what she was doing. The grandmother said Rose sometimes smelled of alcohol when she came home.

I interviewed Rose. She was just a kid, pretty and immature. Still, she had a level of sophistication beyond her years. She tried to manipulate the situation by acting older than she was, hinting at rewards if I didn't push her too hard. I was sure this eleven-year-old little girl was being exploited.

Eventually, the morality her grandmother had instilled in her won out, and Rose gave it all up. A white man in a blue truck with a white cap had stopped her on the street and asked her if she had any friends who liked to party. In spite of having some reservations, Rose said yes and went and got her two best friends. The man took them to a local motel. Using tried and true pedophile techniques of building self-esteem and providing rewards, he got them to undress and pose. He gave them money, cigarettes, and alcohol and made arrangements to meet them again.

This went on for a couple of months. The man lived out of town and only came in on the weekends. Every Friday, Rose and her friends would meet this man. If her best friends were not available, Rose would recruit new ones. Rose was ashamed, however she was not totally willing to part with the money and advantage she had gained. She reluctantly provided a statement and the names of the other girls.

Of the five girls, only two co-operated, and again they were the ones who lived with their grandparents. I got statements. I did not have a name for my suspect. They only knew his first name. I had a description and a pattern. All the girls described the suspect as an older white man, but when you're ten to twelve years old, everyone is old. The suspect had brown hair and faded tattoos. He drove a blue truck with white cap. I was able to identify the motel from the girls' description. I went to the motel and spoke with the staff, who told me about a male matching the description who came in every Friday and provided me with a name.

It was a Friday day shift when I felt I had enough evidence to arrest my suspect. I had not told anyone else in the Saskatoon Police Service about what I was doing because I was experienced enough by then to know I would probably be shut down. Based on my experiences in the first years of my career, I knew that the care factor for my victims would be minimal. Poor people's problems rarely excite the majority other than to reinforce stereotypes they already have about them.

I went to the motel parking lot and waited. I got a call from Communications relaying a message from the inspector, who wanted me to come in so night shift could have my car. I answered that I was tied up but would be in shortly. I had not asked for overtime, nor would I. I did not know if the girls had warned off my suspect or if the motel staff had inadvertently warned him about the police asking questions.

I waited. I got a couple more radio calls asking me to bring in the patrol car. I ignored them, but I knew that I was running out of time. I was about to give up when a blue truck with a white cap pulled into the parking lot. I watched as my suspect got out of his truck to go to his room. Based on the description provided by the girls, I knew that this was my guy. I approached him and arrested him. From his reaction and body language, I knew that I had the right guy. There were no arguments, no impassioned pleas of innocence or outrage. He simply said, "I want a lawyer." I brought him in, booked him, and left my reports. I waited to see how it would all play out.

I went on to my night shifts, and they were busy. I did not hear anything from my inspector or staff sergeant. It was like it had never happened. I found out that my suspect, whom I had charged with three counts of sexual exploitation and three counts of making an invitation for the purpose of sexual touching, had pleaded guilty and had received a five-month jail sentence. At most, he would have to serve three months and he would be out.

I could not believe the leniency of the sentence. He had pleaded guilty to exploiting three young girls, and this sentence was the best we could do? I could not help thinking that if the victims had been three young white girls from suburbia he would have received a lengthy prison term in a federal prison.

I was so angry. Life has since taught me when you are angry it is better to wait before you speak. This was before I learned that lesson. I confronted the crown prosecutor. She became very angry when I suggested that the sentence was too lenient and defensive when I suggested that if the victims had been white the outcome would have been very different. It led to a very heated exchange.

I don't know if I was being fair as there were so many other factors involved in sentencing. At the end of it all, you be the judge: A white man, represented by a lawyer, before a judge, negotiates a sentence of five months for luring pre-teens into prostitution and then sexually exploiting them. The girls were never given a chance to have their stories heard. Fair? I don't know, just saying…

All five of the girls went on to a life of prostitution and drugs. I lost track of four of them. My little freckled-faced Rose broke out of the cycle and picked alcohol as an addiction. In the summer of 2012, I arrested Rose on an outstanding warrant for assault. Sad is only word I have. We had a chance as a society to save these girls, and we missed it.

In the Riversdale neighbourhood of Saskatoon there is another inner-city school, more modern in architecture, probably built in the fifties or early sixties. One block from that school lurked another pedophile. I received a call from another grandmother that her two grandchildren, aged eight and eleven, had been acting strangely and now had money she had never given them. She had heard from Rose's grandmother that I had helped her.

I went to their home and met two shy little girls. My initial interviews with them were awkward. These were children in the true sense of the word. They knew that they had been caught doing something, and they were defensive. I tried to explain to them that they were not in trouble. I told them that someone else might be, but whatever happened was not their fault. Before I could even get to what had happened to them, they told me that other kids were doing the same thing. It took a while to find out what the same thing was, but eventually the girls told the story.

There was an older white man who lived a block away from the school. He saw them walking and asked if they wanted to see his turtle. Both the girls, never having seen a turtle before, said yes. The male invited them to his apartment and gave them hot chocolate and candies. He also gave them pocket change. He told them they could come back anytime and they could bring their friends. This had gone on for a couple of weeks, and nothing sexual appeared to have happened. By this time, the male was well known to the children in the neighbourhood. One of the girls even referred to him as her boyfriend.

I did a series of interviews with these kids, which I videotaped. I was concerned about the interviews because it was so easy to suggest things to kids or for them to say things just to please the interviewer. During interviews the kids revealed that the suspect would take a shower when they were there and then accidentally drop his towel. After a while, the children got used to his nakedness, and then he upped the ante.

By this time, I had a good idea who my suspect was and what was in his apartment. Coupled with the statements, I had enough to get a search warrant and arrest him. After I obtained the warrant, another constable and I went to his home and arrested him. He matched the description the kids had provided perfectly, and everything the kids said would be there was, including the now notorious turtle. The suspect was fifty-one years old.

I was elated. My contempt for him was on my sleeve, and I could not hide my feelings. He was transported to detention, and then I laid a slew of charges on him.

I was so angry. In retrospect, I should've let someone else interview him. I did not. A confession would have sealed the deal and saved the children from testifying. I blew it. When I went in the room, I knew from the outset that there would be no rapport. I just hated this person front of me, and he knew it. He also knew I could not legally kill him. He merely stated, "My lawyer told me not to say anything." We were done.

For some reason, they scheduled the preliminary hearing for when I was on holidays. Some detectives have been assigned follow-up. I got back from holidays and one of the detectives told me that the charges had been stayed because the girls would not testify. The crown prosecutor told me that the interviews were good but they could not proceed on videotaped interviews alone. The girls needed to testify as to what had happened. My suspect was free.

He moved out of the community, and the last I heard he was living with a woman who had children. This case was twenty years ago as of 2013. Hopefully, he's occupying the special place in hell reserved for people like him.

I learned a lot about my own ego, arrogance, and overconfidence.

Since these cases, there's been a total revamping of how police investigate sexual crimes against children. There were several high-profile cases in Canada and the United States where wild accusations of cults and ritual sexual abuse were investigated and then fell apart at trial. Children were always at the center of it all, and police techniques were severely criticized. Now all investigators are specially trained and work in conjunction with psychologists and social workers. The crown prosecutors review each case, and the whole system is engaged from start to finish before any charges are laid. Turtle man would have been toast.

Part of being a police officer is the ability to move on. I have, and I have learned. But I have never forgotten those children.

There are some things we deal with where there is no applicable law. One morning in January 2011, a call came in of children running down the street asking for help because their mother was dead. Several units responded. I got there second and walked into a messy two-storey house. I was directed by the original caller to go to the basement. On the floor of the basement was a woman, obviously dead, with a ligature around her neck. The young man who had called told us that the children had run up to him as he was scraping his windshield, asking for help because their mother was hanging in the basement. He went into the house and called 911 and then cut her down as he was instructed by the ambulance dispatcher.

While he was doing this, the children kept running toward the home of a friend of their mother. They were crying and hysterical. After their horrific discovery, they had run from the house inadequately dressed for the bitter January temperatures. Another sergeant and a constable found them. They put them in their cars and tried to find out what had happened.

I stayed at the scene and secured it until detectives and the Forensic Identification section processed the scene. The other sergeant and the constable who had the kids took them to the address they had been running to. There they learned that there was a boyfriend who had been in the home the previous night. The detectives wanted to find him and find out what he knew. They were trying to establish the chain of events leading to the woman's death.

I found some identification in a male's name in the bedroom on the second floor. I passed the name along and stayed at the house until the woman's body was removed. The officers who were with the children bought them some lunch and stayed with them until a relative from out of town came to take custody of them. As callous as this sounds, I actually had the easier job. Living survivors, especially children, are more emotionally draining than dealing with a dead body.

It turned out that the name on the identification I found was an alias, and the detectives found the real name for the boyfriend. The death had occurred on our last day shift. The detective sergeant in charge of the file asked if I could locate the boyfriend on our night shift. At this point, I was convinced that the boyfriend had found the woman hanging and had left her there for the children to find. It was not long before I found him, using information the lead investigator had given me. When we first made contact with him, he was unco-operative. The contempt I felt for him was pretty clear. Ultimately, he was detained and transported to the police service headquarters for an interview with the investigators. After they were done, he was released. There was no charge applicable. He had found a woman hanging and let her children find her.

There was not a thing we could do about it. At the end of the day, where do you put that kind of anger and frustration?

5.

A Sense of Belonging

When I got home with my enlistment papers, my mother was reluctant to sign them. I argued that this would be a good opportunity for me and painted an alternative picture of me, a high school dropout, working as a labourer for the rest of my life. My mother relented and signed.

I took the train back to North Bay and, with new orders, went to Ottawa to wait for a flight to CFB Cornwallis, which used to be the Canadian Forces basic training base in Nova Scotia. I spent one night at the Uplands Air Force Base in the transit barracks. I still had my long hair, and the soldiers on the base snickered and made comments under their breath when they saw me, starting what would be my lifelong contempt for rear echelon people.

I took the flight from Ottawa to Halifax. Once in Halifax, I began to meet the other recruits from all over Canada as we boarded a bus bound for CFB Cornwallis. The atmosphere on the bus was nervous and anxious. All of us were wondering what we had gotten ourselves into. Almost all of us had long hair and were dressed in jeans, jean jackets, and T-shirts. Only one or two of the guys were wearing dress shirts and slacks. Newfoundlanders, prairie boys, and city dwellers, we were a good mix. There was only one other native guy. He was from Alberta.

We arrived at Cornwallis and debussed. We were formed into lines by three or four tough-looking NCOs. There was a lot of yelling and swearing.

The senior NCO usually picks one recruit and makes example out of him. He picks on the recruit relentlessly until the recruit packs it in. The NCO does this to toughen up the other recruits. The chosen recruit is deemed to be a necessary casualty. I was that recruit.

In basic training, when you are the chosen recruit to be sacrificed, the other trainees instinctively draw away from you. They know that you are a marked man and you will not be there for long.

I was struggling with drill and failing to pass inspection after inspection by week four. I was going to be re-coursed if I failed one more inspection. Being re-coursed meant going back and having to repeat two weeks of training. In basic training, two weeks was like two years. One day, just before the morning inspection, we were rushing around doing final checks when one of the recruits on a broom swept everything under my bed. Everyone knew what he had done. There was no time to get rid of it, as I could hear the boots of the NCOs coming upstairs.

I was re-coursed. For the next eleven weeks, I was on every extra duty and remedial training available.

I never received a coveted leave pass throughout basic training. I would be on parade on Friday afternoons and the NCOs would call out soldiers' names and they would march out to receive their leave pass and then fall out. Week after week, I would be the only guy still standing at attention when all the passes had been handed out. The sergeant would ask me what I was waiting for and then give me my weekend duties.

I was in week eight when I almost broke. I called my mother in Northern Ontario and asked if I could come home. My mother said no and told me to finish what I started. Years later, I saw movie called *An Officer and a Gentleman*. In one scene, the drill sergeant was trying to get a candidate to quit. The recruit yelled back in despair to the drill sergeant, "I've got no place else to go!" I could relate, and in the long run was glad my mother had said no.

A tribute to the strength of my mother's character and the force of her personality is how all of us turned out. She gave us the drive we needed to succeed. My older brother has been working with mentally challenged and autistic children for more than thirty years. My younger brother is the vice president of scripted programming for Frantic Films in Toronto, and my little sister is a police officer. Sadly, my sister from my father's second marriage was killed in a traffic accident in 1997.

When we got past the marching and the spit and polish and started to use weapons and learn fieldcraft, I started to turn things around.

We started basic training with 125 men, and thirteen weeks later, there were 45 of us remaining.

When I graduated from basic training, I was posted to the Princess

Patricia's Canadian Light Infantry battle school at CFB Wainwright, Alberta. Now I was in my element—the battle school was what I had signed up for. I had the good fortune of being assigned to Master Corporal Spellen's rifle section.

Master Corporal Spellen was a natural leader. He was a no-nonsense soldier, dedicated and well spoken. He taught me how to be a soldier. Years later, he told me that we were the first course he had taught at battle school. I was shocked because he was so good. A tribute to the man's leadership ability is the fact that from his first course, he produced my friend Chris White, who went on to become the command regimental sergeant major of the Canadian Forces, two sergeant majors, a warrant officer, and a police officer.

I understood—and understand even better now—that the process during basic training was to break you down as an individual and make you a team player. As much as I hated the drill and inspections, I understood their necessity to make you better organized and react instinctively to verbal orders under stress. I got two weeks extra training in basic training because I was not much for shining and marching, but we started the sixteen-week battle school course with a clean slate. At battle school, it was ability, not shine, that mattered.

I loved battle school. I learned to use the various weapons of the infantry: mortars, machine guns, and grenades. I learned patrol techniques. I learned how to use the radios. I learned basic tactics and was tested physically as I had never been tested before. Master Corporal Spellen laid the groundwork and set the mould for the leadership style I would try to emulate: Make no excuses and get the job done. Eat last, sleep last, and put others ahead of yourself if you are in charge.

When I graduated after sixteen weeks, there were twenty-three candidates remaining. I hoped that the grandfather I was named after, a corporal who was killed in the Second World War with Lake Superior Regiment in Europe, could see me, and that he would be proud.

We were posted to the second battalion of the Princess Patricia's Canadian Light Infantry at CFB Winnipeg. The second battalion was a mechanized unit. We were equipped with armoured personnel carriers.

I was so proud. I loved being a soldier, even though these were the lean years for the Canadian Forces. Every branch of the service was under strength, especially the combat arms infantry, armour, artillery, and the combat engineers. Our equipment was for the most part Vietnam era and was in desperate need of modernization. All of that did not matter to me. I was a soldier in a regiment with a proud history and believed that if push came to shove, we could do our duty. In truth, our life expectancy in a combat environment would have been very short. I never felt more privileged.

The Canadian Armed Forces in 1978 had fewer personnel than the Canadian National Railway. It had been merged from the three services—the army, navy, and air forc—into one service. The distinctive uniforms of each were traded in for one uniform. What I didn't know when I joined was how low morale was. The Vietnam War had just recently ended, and soldiers and soldiering were not all that popular. Respective governments had cut defence spending drastically year after year. The military was usually the first place government looked when it went looking for more treasure.

I believe the Canadian government's commitment to international peacekeeping was the only thing that kept the forces from being further reduced in the late seventies. The Canadian government, having committed the country to international peacekeeping, could not pull out without a major loss of face. Unwittingly, the government helped staunch the bleeding of the Canadian forces, and even then they tried to do peacekeeping on a shoestring budget.

I was thrown into different leadership roles when a section commander went down and there was no one to replace him. Eventually, I was selected for the section commander's course, without a doubt the toughest course I ever took, bar none. The first course, I made it for fifteen of the seventeen weeks when my sister was injured and I was returned to my unit and went home. My sister recovered, but I would have to redo the course. Before the next course started, I had time to go on a major summer exercise for six weeks and then back to another section commander's course.

The course was designed to make combat leaders. In the field portions of the course, if you failed to give orders properly or failed to be decisive in attacks, withdrawals, or the setting up of the defence positions, you failed. You were done, returned to your unit, and possibly never given the chance to take the course again. Sleep deprivation and stress were the tools used to see if you could deal with adverse conditions and keep your presence of mind as a leader. Sixty-five of us started on the course, and six of us graduated. I was promoted on our graduation parade. I went up two ranks, private to corporal one day, and corporal to master corporal the next.

I had been in the reconnaissance platoon for a couple of years by then and stayed there as a detachment commander after I was promoted. About a year later, I was deployed overseas to Cyprus.

For over twenty-nine years, thousands of Canadian soldiers have served in Cyprus on peacekeeping missions. Twenty-eight Canadian soldiers were killed there. Yet most Canadians, and especially the young ones, have no idea where Cyprus even is.

Cyprus is a small island in the northwest corner of the Mediterranean Sea populated by about 900,000 Greeks and Turks. It is beautiful island that unfortunately is still divided between the Greeks and Turks after two wars. After the first war, the United Nations stepped in and enforced the ceasefire and still deploys peacekeepers to physically keep the Turks and Greeks separated.

I was deployed there from October 1982 until March 1983. I was a twenty-one-year-old master corporal with the reconnaissance platoon. We landed at a British air force base in Larnaca. We deplaned and boarded buses. From there, we were driven at breakneck speeds to Ledra Palace in the centre of Nicosia, the capital city of the Greek government. The palace used to be a five-star luxury hotel until it was seized and fortified by Canadian soldiers during the last war in 1974. Ledra Palace became one of the operating bases for the Canadian peacekeeping mission.

We were tired from the flight, and I fully expected we would have a gradual and orderly changeover with the artillery and armoured units we were taking over from. Instead, I was told to have my men find their rooms, store their gear, and report to the reconnaissance platoon building immediately.

Once we were there, two NCOs for the Lord Strathcona's Horse, an armoured reconnaissance unit, showed us our jeeps. The jeeps were just like the ones from the old television show "The Rat Patrol." Each one had a machine gun and a radio. They were painted white and had a large blue United Nations flag attached to the radio antenna. The NCOs had the other section commanders and me jump in the jeeps in the communicator spots. They took us on a whirlwind tour of the line. They told us where the danger spots and checkpoints were. I was trying to take everything in—the heat, the dust, and the smells. The strangeness of riding in a jeep between two groups of armed men who were technically still at war made me uneasy. War-damaged buildings and improvised fortifications mixed with a foreign architecture flew past us. I am sure we set a patrol land speed record doing the patrol. We pulled back into the reconnaissance platoon compound, and the NCOs from the Lord Strat's told us that the next patrol was at night. There was so much information to absorb. I called my guys together to start to check our weapons and familiarize ourselves with the standard operating procedures we would be adopting. After I was satisfied, I sent them off to eat and grab a few hours of sleep before the next patrol.

When the appointed time came for our first night patrol, I had been up for more than twenty-four hours. While my guys had been sleeping, I had been studying the maps and learning where everything was. Still I felt woefully unprepared, and I couldn't wait for the guys from Strathcona's to give me more information.

My guys reported to the reconnaissance compound and started checking the vehicles, their radios and weapons. When the appointed hour for the patrol came, we were the only ones there. I sent one of the guys find the NCOs or an officer of the Strathcona's. He came back from the palace with a look of dismay and told me they were gone back to Canada. We were on our own.

Our first solo patrol was at night in a foreign country between two armies whose island we had just come to. I had been told that the Greeks and Turks would test us during the first couple of weeks of our tour to see how professional we were. To top everything off, the jeeps had standard transmissions and were old. The clutches had minds of their own, and I had two inexperienced young drivers. We lurched and jumped through the first couple of miles and almost created an international incident when my driver almost hit a Greek checkpoint. They came out yelling and pointing their guns at us. We stone-faced them and carried on with the patrol. Somehow we made it through without getting ourselves killed or starting a war. After an adrenaline-filled couple of hours, we got back to the compound and stored our gear. I sat down to write my report and realized how much I did not know.

It was one of the best lessons I've ever learned about professionalism. When you think you are trained and mission-ready, train harder. The lack of preparation for the transition between our two reconnaissance units shocked me. A lot of it came from the ranks above us—the majority of the officers and senior NCOs had been on multiple tours, and I don't believe they took the mission as seriously as they should have. I remember thinking that the complacency of our unit and the lack of information-sharing would have quickly led to the destruction of our unit if serious fighting had ever broken out. If there were plans in place, they were not shared with the junior NCOs, and if the people with the plans were taken out early, it would have been a mess. It was like everyone had forgotten the old army saying, "Fail to plan, you plan to fail." I'm not saying that all the soldiers deployed were not professionals. Many of them were career soldiers and had dedicated their lives to the army. I think the lack of commitment from the government permeated all aspects of the military in the late seventies and eighties.

After I was out of the service and with the Saskatoon police, I watched as my old unit was deployed to the former Yugoslavia, and I hoped they were better equipped and better prepared than we were when we were in Cyprus. I learned that if you're going to make a commitment, make a commitment. Half measures will never do.

I stayed in the reconnaissance platoon after we returned to Canada, went on to the rifle team, instructed on courses, and enjoyed almost every minute of it. The beauty of the military for me was the way all the native stereotypes I dealt with now worked in my favour. It was assumed that I was a natural soldier, never got lost, never had to eat, and had natural abilities in the field. Ability and merit were the rollers your career moved on.

All in all though, there was something missing. There was not enough action. The Canadian Forces were big on peacekeeping, and while peacekeeping had challenges and elements of danger, it just wasn't enough. There was also a sense of a lack of commitment from the government to the military. It seemed we did things halfheartedly. The soldiers were professional, but the civilians in charge were not. I briefly considered joining the United States Army and even the French Foreign Legion, but I am Canadian and I love my country, so I didn't really consider it for long. I re-mustered to the military police.

The army and all of the armed forces trades are available to anyone who is physically and mentally up to the challenge. I say *carpe diem* to anyone who is even considering joining. Until you feel the pride of earning the right to wear the uniform of the service defending our country, you will never know what you are capable of.

I served with the military from 11 December 1978 until I was honourably discharged in March 1987. There are so many things I remember fondly about the service which help me forget the less pleasant aspects.

The pride of achievement stands out. I have vivid recollections of my time in the service, I think because of its intensity. The smell of the earth as you are standing in a trench, and the smell of gun oil and shoe polish in a clean barracks. I loved the sound of the metallic clinking of empty casings being ejected, the deep, throaty rumble of a heavy machine gun firing, and links falling to the ground when on the firing range. I loved being with comrades on leave in a foreign country, and warm spring days when I would walk out of the barracks, put on my beret, and check my uniform while listening to the drums and bagpipes warming up before I marched out onto the parade square. Being part of something and having a sense of belonging was just what I needed to help me move on to the next chapter of my life.

6.

No Ammunition Is Ever Surplus

I was posted to CFB Borden and started a seventeen-week military police course. It was a strange feeling not being part of a unit. The infantry had an identity of its own, and everything was done for the benefit of the regiment. This training and my subsequent duties would find me working on my own or with a partner.

I graduated as the top candidate on my course, and to my surprise I was posted to CFB Wainwright, Alberta. I had already spent seventeen weeks there in battle school and countless months there on exercises with the infantry. I knew all too well what type of base Wainwright was: a training base built in World War II with a small permanent staff and large transient population of soldiers on exercises and training. I had hoped to go somewhere different, but that was the hand I was dealt, and I resolved to make the best of it.

As I expected, Wainwright was a rough-and-tumble place, with lots of bar fights, impaired drivers, and violent crimes. I was back in my element once again. I was getting lots of good cases, and there was never a shortage of work.

There was a pervasive attitude of live and let live on the base. Impaired driving was commonplace. There was an attitude among the civilian employees that if you needed materials from the base you could just take them at the end of the workday. There were twelve military police on base, and very few charges were ever laid. The local RCMP detachment and the NCO in charge of it had little time for us and our low level of professionalism.

Within four months, I laid at least eighty charges for domestic assault, impaired driving, and theft. I started to do checks at the main gate of the base, and if a civilian employee had Department of National Defence material in their possession, I would make them return it to their workplace. If I caught them a second time, I would charge them. The first time I stopped soldiers who were impaired, I would give them a twenty-four-hour suspension; if I stopped them again, I would charge them under the *Criminal Code* and bring them to the local RCMP detachment for a breath test. Once the RCMP was involved, the military could not sweep it under the rug. I caused a lot of tension in our section and on the base because this apparently was not the way we did business. The base security officer called me in and told me to stop charging military personal with impaired driving. I put my notebook on his desk and told him that if he wrote the order in there, I would. He told me to get out of his office and put me on night shifts for the next six months.

The other MPs began to take part, and apart from the people who liked the previous way of doing things, the personnel on the base began to have more respect for the military police and the law. We developed a good working relationship with the local RCMP and, except for our respective commanders, became good friends.

I had been there for about nine months when I rolled my ankle during a soccer game. It was badly sprained, so I was assigned to man the front desk of the guardhouse. Answering the phone, issuing permits, and directing people was not very exciting, but one afternoon I answered the phone and at the other end was a constable from the Edmonton Police Service. He explained that part of his beat included a store that was selling military ammunition—7.62-mm rifle and machine-gun rounds and 9-mm pistol and submachine-gun rounds—out of forty-five-gallon drums at a surprising discount. He inquired as to when military ammunition was declared surplus. I told him that to the best of my knowledge military ammunition was never surplus, that if it were, it would be destroyed, and that I would get back to him.

I made some inquiries with my sergeant. He answered, "No ammunition is ever surplus," looked at me like I was stupid, and that was the end of it.

By that time, I was almost healed and able to head back on the road. I met a civilian friend at a local restaurant, a good, solid, honest man. I told him about the phone call and my suspicions that the ammunition was coming from our base—Wainwright was the largest training base in western Canada, the home of the PPCLI Battle School, and millions of rounds of ammunition were expended there every year. I told him about my sergeant's disinterest and expressed my frustration.

He told me that he was opening a gun shop in a small town outside Wainwright and that he would put the word out that he would buy military ammunition. He wanted to advance his career, and this would definitely help. The next couple of months were to be a five-coupon ride. My friend set up a shop, put out the word, and soon ammunition began to come in. He had a video camera set up and captured all the transactions. The suspects knew it was there, thought it was a good idea to have a video set up in a gun shop, and never gave it a second thought.

Senior noncommissioned officers were taking a percentage of the ammunition allotted for training and selling it off base to civilians. I was doing this on my own. I didn't know who to trust. I collected the ammunition my friend had purchased and stored it in an unused cell in the old wing of the guardhouse. I started using my own money to reimburse my friend, but soon enough it was out of hand and I was broke. I was not sure how to proceed—this was going to be a major case.

As a soldier, it went against everything I believed in, and even worse, these were soldiers I trained with and respected, men who had served their country for years and who were now charged with training recruits. What motivates someone to do something like this? Who thought of it, and how did professional soldiers come to take part in it?

I was overwhelmed. I had to tell someone. The plainclothes investigator in our section never really interacted with the uniformed guys, and admittedly it was a mystery to me what he did every day. I approached him and basically laid out everything that had happened up to that point. His face lit up. He was so excited—in the nine months I had been there I'd never seen him so engaged. It struck me that he saw this as an opportunity. This would be a career changer for him. I was saddened by it all and knew the outcome would be life-changing for a lot of people: careers, marriages, and prison time. This was nothing to be happy about.

The investigator hatched a plan so that we could prove which NCOs were bringing ammunition from which allotment. It was simple but labour-intensive: I went into the ammunition bunkers and painted each allotment with different coloured invisible ink. Of course no one else could know, and I could not trip the alarms. I also had to stay on regular patrol rotation so no one would question where I was or what I was doing. I was not getting a lot of sleep, and I worried constantly that the investigation would be discovered before we knew the extent of the corruption. Even though Wainwright was a huge sprawling base, the permanent staff was small, and it was hard to keep secrets. I ate in the same mess as some of soldiers we were investigating. I slept in the same barracks. I was so sleep deprived, I developed a twitch in my eye.

Eventually, we used up our unit's resources. The investigator said we needed outside help. We were a subordinate unit to 1MP platoon out of Calgary. Our investigator contacted them, and in no time several investigators were on our base. Same as our investigator, these guys were excited. This was a career-changing case—everyone knew it. No one seemed to care about the damage it would cause. I had mixed feelings and felt the Judas.

At this point in the investigation, I began to get pushed out. I had fewer tasks and was no longer part of the briefings as the case progressed, but my friend continued to co-operate and still met me to exchange information.

The breadth and scope of the investigation had changed several times. The offenders were aware that some of the ammunition might have found its way to a white supremacist group. Other materials were leaving the base: combat clothing, webbing, and sought-after military goods. Our parent unit used up all of its resources and were in turn obligated to call National Defence headquarters. Now the big guns came in. An elite military police undercover investigative unit arrived but did not set foot on the base.

The senior officer of this unit during the briefing on the case asked me how much experience I had, and when I told him, he promptly told me I was off the case. I was relieved. I was exhausted, and tension had taken its toll. I do not think I had had a day off since this all started. Like a good soldier, I went to a local bar and started pounding. There were way too many egos in play now, and I wanted no part of it. My friend, after hearing I had been removed from the case, insisted that I be brought back in. So I was, hangover and all, the very next day.

Ottawa, worried about the extent of the case and the possibility that more serious or heavier weapons could bleed from the base, ordered everyone identified to be arrested in a base-wide round up. The operation was carefully planned, and within a few hours everyone involved was in custody. When I made my assigned arrest, an NCO, he told me to do my job the way I had been taught. It's a soldier thing, like going in front of a firing squad without a blindfold. There was lots of high-fives and backslapping. I was not included and was glad not to have been. All I saw was pain and shame on the faces of proud soldiers who had made a terrible mistake for the sake of a few dollars.

Several weeks later, a court-martial was convened. Prior to the beginning of the proceedings, all the charged parties pleaded guilty, saving the forces from embarrassment and keeping the whole affair out of the public eye. There were several promotions, including our base investigator, who was promoted and posted to Germany, out of what he considered to be a backwater base. Almost everyone involved came out okay when all was said and done. The infantry NCOs were jailed and demoted but not released. They came back, re-earned their rank, and went on to serve with distinction in Yugoslavia and other theatres.

I stuck it out on patrol in Wainwright for another year and applied to the Saskatoon Police Service.

My assessment read that I had been involved in nine major cases while in my first year with the military police. I learned a lot while I was there, not all of it good. I was living off base with a member of the RCMP when I decided I wanted to try civilian policing. At first I told him that I was interested in the Mounties. He quickly discouraged me as they had been dealing with a pay freeze for a couple of years. He suggested the Saskatoon Police Service, and added that they had a good reputation.

After I applied to the Saskatoon police and went through the selection process, I had to come to Saskatoon for my final interview. I didn't have a suit. I had never needed one. Anything formal I needed to attend, I just went in uniform. So the morning of my interview, I was in Saskatoon without a suit. I went to the Army and Navy Store and bought the most god-awful chocolate brown polyester suit and ill-fitting shoes off the racks. The suit smelled like a cheap shower curtain after you take it out of the bag. I'm glad I do not have any pictures, and I cannot believe they hired me. I was still in the bush league.

My military police badge (courtesy the author)

7.

Leadership, Ego, and Arrogance

You can always tell how serious a call is by the tone of the dispatcher. You can also hear the 911 calls coming in behind her. Experience fires an extra shot of adrenaline into you as you acknowledge the call and turn your vehicle and your thoughts toward it. You imagine the worst and hope for the best. If you're the first unit to arrive, you have to take a second to realize what you're seeing so your brain can absorb the shock and formulate a plan.

If you're the second or third unit to arrive, you can tell from the voices of the officers on the radio the seriousness of the tragedy as it unfolds. You hear urgent and clipped transmissions by police officers troubled by what they are seeing, looking for direction and leadership to start to do what they've been trained to do.

When you're the senior officer or the sergeant and you roll up on the call, the patrolmen look at you relieved and reassured. You get out and take it all in. Your goal is to preserve life, protect life, and gain control. You ask for whatever assistance is required, restore order, and no matter how serious the situation, except for the technical investigation, in an hour or two it's like it never happened. Traffic is reopened, firefighters have swept up the debris, and the ambulances are gone. The crime scene tape may still be up, but the urgency is gone. There is nothing left to do except try to process what you have seen and done. And that, my friend, is often the hardest part.

Not everything police do is dramatic or traumatic. There are long, quiet nights and uneventful days. It is not always what police do, but rather what we expect police to do. We—and rightfully so—expect police to be ready to respond to whatever calamities life throws our way. We expect a professional and measured response to emergencies. We expect the police will be there.

A police officer does not have the luxury of walking away from a problem. As a police sergeant, one of the things that got my blood boiling was when an officer would throw up his hands and ask, "What do you expect us to do?" As a police officer, you are the leader when you have been called to a situation. Do something! Take action where required, provide alternatives, and provide leadership. Sometimes, just a calm reassurance is enough to resolve an issue.

There is no perfect organization, especially in policing. Policing is all about working with people. Each constable is different. Each constable will experience different things at different times in their career. The experiences they have might be unique to them due to circumstances, and no other officer might ever experience the same type of thing.

There's a leader in all of us. Sometimes, your ability to lead is just about the time and the place—you find yourself in a position where you have to take charge, and your training and confidence kick in and all of a sudden you *are* in charge. It has been said many times that to be a good leader, you must be a good follower first. The reason it has been said many times is because it is true. Police, like any other professional, must learn their trade. The initial training is only a vessel for experience to fill. As a police officer, you can never stop learning. You have the obligation to the community to learn all you can.

Can you teach leadership? Yes, you can, but one of the facts of taught leadership is that it has to be unlocked using the keys of training, experience, and acquired confidence. Most leaders at one point in their lives were passive followers until those tumblers lined up.

I tell new constables fresh out of police college that when they are called to and roll up on a traumatic or violent event, no one knows except themselves that they are new to policing. People want them to restore order and take control. People want them to return things as close as possible to normal. It is a lot to ask of a young man or woman. It is, however, the nature of the beast. On their first day alone on the street, a twenty-three year old can be the first officer at a murder scene and have to deal with screaming family members, a crime scene, and possibly suspects. Mental preparation and clearly stated expectations of what is required are what I try to give to new constables.

You have to practise what you preach. For years, I shamelessly took the best methods of good leaders. I analyzed bad leaders and what made them bad. As a young police officer, it is but one of the many duties that you need to master: to lead as fearlessly as possible, remembering always that people see everything you do both on and off duty.

There are many basic principles of leadership. They are timeless for a reason, and a leader who discounts these principles does so at his or her own peril: Lead by example. Master your craft or trade. Identify leaders and train your replacement. Put the needs of your people before your own. Never stop learning. There are many more, and so much has been written about leadership that serious students could spend all their time reading and never really lead anyone.

There are two types of leadership positions. The first one is positional—those who have achieved a rank and are appointed to a position of leadership. The second is natural—people who, by deeds or action, are recognized by their peers as the leader. I have worked with both types, and I prefer the latter.

The biggest obstacles placed in front of any leader of police or any other occupation are ego, fear of failure, and self-preservation. These obstacles are put there by the potential leader themselves. Ego and arrogance have been the downfall of many good people and many potentially good leaders. They are especially poor traits to have if you are a police officer or police leader. Ego and arrogance are the sworn enemies of good police officers and always will be.

Quiet confidence is the remedy. Good leaders know their craft, and if they do not, they learn and draw on the experience of others freely until they do. I have worked with a lot of people in my life. Men and women, brave and faint-hearted, leaders and followers, I took something from them all. Everyone has something to offer. At the same time, I've always wondered why it was so difficult for police services to ask the rank-and-file officers for ideas. Strong leadership is not threatened by asking for ideas. Strong leadership tries new things, and if they don't work out, learn from it and try something else.

Over the years, I have seen too many people make decisions quickly, based on their positional authority and backed by their ego, which with a moment of quiet reflection they would have known were wrong. Once the wrong decision was made and identified as wrong, these leaders' ego and arrogance would not let them change course and remedy the situation. Letting your ego chart your path and being arrogant are the fastest way to lose the confidence and respect of the people you lead, and if you lose their confidence because of these traits, you will never get it back.

I had been on the same platoon for fifteen years when a new staff sergeant was transferred in. The staff sergeant was coming to a strong platoon. Our platoon was experienced and led the platoons in arrests and productivity. Morale was good, and everyone worked well together at the constable level. Some of the junior officers asked about the new watch commander and what he was like. I told them I thought he was capable and knew that he had a good investigative background. I also knew that he was an ambitious man, and that this position was a stepping stone and an opportunity for him to show his leadership abilities.

I thought the new staff sergeant would come to our shift and learn who we were and what we are all about. Unfortunately, on our first parade he chose to cut against the grain. As I recall, he came out, took the podium, and proceeded to tell us how poorly we were doing, how we needed more discipline, and how he was going to fix us. I watched the other officers as he spoke. Bewilderment, anger, and resentment were clearly etched on their faces, and I hoped they would hold their tongues until they were out of the staff sergeant's hearing range.

We worked for him because we had to, and we worked out of personal pride. We worked in spite of him and those who joined his camp. Trust in a leader can be that transient and fragile. Ultimately, the relationship between us never healed from that first day.

Our job as leaders is to ensure that we know and care for the welfare of our people. We need to give them the tools they need to do their job. They have a difficult enough job to do and don't need sarcastic, mean-spirited, and ineffective leadership. We as police leaders owe them that. They, in turn, will take the leadership they see from their leaders and provide that leadership to the people we serve.

Lead by example and make a stand when you know you're right if you want to be a good leader.

In 2004, my partner and I, working in separate cars on a day shift, responded to a frantic and tragic call. A twelve-year-old boy had been found hanging. We both had twelve-year-old sons at the time. The paramedics arrived about the same time we did and immediately launched into efforts to save the boy's life.

The boy had been found by his teenage sister. Her anguish and grief overwhelmed us as we tried to establish what had happened. As we were trying to establish the sequence of events and get the situation under control, the parents came home. The paramedics, God bless them, were still trying to revive the boy. It was a frantic scene, and everyone's face showed the strain and horror we felt. I had to hold both of the parents back from going into the house. My heart was breaking with grief for them, for their confusion, raw pain, and sorrow, when another constable came up to the scene. I thought he had more information or directions from the sergeant, who was still in his vehicle, conveniently parked half a block down the street. I stepped aside with him.

The constable told me—reluctantly because he knew how outrageous the message was—that the sergeant wanted to know if I needed all the officers who were there.

I was enraged. I told the constable to go back and tell the sergeant that it would be better if he were gone by the time I got to the station. The constable swallowed and went to the sergeant's vehicle. I do not know what the constable said exactly, but sergeant drove away and left us to deal with this unfolding tragedy without the benefit of his leadership.

The paramedics, still frantically working on the boy, evacuated him to the hospital. I cleared the house and went to the hospital once our forensics officers arrived, but I knew in my heart that the boy had died at the house in spite of the best efforts of the paramedics. At the hospital, I met with the parents.

Their son had died. They looked to me for answers. Their eyes were piercing. I could not imagine the hopelessness they were feeling or the utter despair and frustration enveloping them. I cannot help thinking that this was the sergeant's job. I told them that the coroner would be conducting the investigation from this point on. I told them that their son's hanging could have been an accident. Then I left.

There is no pain as great as the parent's loss of a child. It leaves you forever marked, and stays with you all of your days.

When I got back to the station, the sergeant was long gone. My partner and I did not know what to say to each other. I don't think a lot of words were necessary. I knew we both felt the same.

The next evening, the staff sergeant told my partner that he, the sergeant, and I were going to have a meeting to discuss what had gone wrong. Mistake. I was still furious and emotional. I could not even look at the sergeant at first—my contempt for him was obvious.

The staff sergeant had me speak first. I was as blunt as I could be. In short, hard clips, I told the sergeant that he was, in my opinion, the worst I had ever seen or worked with. What made it all the more outrageous was that he knew how to do his job, he just chose not to. I did not care if I was charged with insubordination. After I gutted him, I tried to finish on a positive. I told him he had the experience and knowledge necessary to do his job. My partner did the same, and at the end of it the sergeant never said a word to defend himself.

When our one-sided meeting was over, the staff sergeant thanked us for our candour. I was not done yet and told the staff sergeant that he was as much at fault as the sergeant because he knew the sergeant did not do his job and did nothing.

Spent, I left. After seventeen years on my platoon, I knew my time there was over. I transferred to the Street Crime unit shortly afterwards.

I have a basic leadership principle: Nobody comes to work and says at the beginning of the workday, "I'm going to do a bad job." If you start off with this basic premise, you can use it as leverage to get good work out of just about anybody. Bad work is usually the result of laziness, lack of supervision, and lack of clarity. If you come across bad or shoddy work, it's your job as a leader to point it out as soon as you find it and then coach and mentor the employee on how to do it right.

In the police world, the importance of correcting problems immediately is magnified. An officer who starts to take shortcuts or is allowed to bend the rules will become ineffective and a liability.

In January 2012, patrol officers were dispatched to a domestic dispute involving a wanted parole violator. I started to head into the area in case they needed backup. One of the officers was a recruit still in field training with less than two months on the street. As the officers were arriving, I heard the recruit over the radio saying that the suspect was fleeing on foot. I went to take a perimeter position until our K-9 officer arrived. A moment later, I heard frantic calls for assistance at the house where the suspect was supposed to have fled from. My heart sank. It sounded like one or more officers were injured. I heard a call for an ambulance. I arrived within a minute and saw three officers incapacitated by bear spray.

Bear spray is a commercially sold chemical irritant meant to spray at bears if they get too close. It is an extremely painful experience to be sprayed. It makes it hard to breathe and burns your eyes. When you're a police officer, being incapacitated is one of your worst nightmares. You cannot defend yourself, and your weapon is vulnerable.

Several other cars arrived on the scene, and the affected officers were taken out of the danger zone. The K-9 officer was still at the front of the house and said the suspect was still inside. We went up the stairs to the front door. The spray still hung thick in the air, making it hard to breathe. I knew I only had a few seconds to get the suspect into custody before the effects of the spray made me ineffective. I started coughing right away. I could see the suspect in the area by the kitchen. I took a breath and went in. The K-9 officer could not come any further than the door because the spray was so thick in the house. The suspect put his hands behind his back when ordered to. I handcuffed him and hustled him outside into the fresh air. There were quite a few officers at the scene now as well as an ambulance. I quickly took the arrested male to my car. Once he was secured, I read him his rights. His only comment was that the cops should have listened to him. I told him he was lucky all he was doing was getting arrested.

My skin was burning from the irritant. I knew it would not be long before it was in my eyes. Another sergeant arrived and was helping the officers who had been sprayed. There were a lot of angry cops, and I thought it best to get my arrest into the station and into a cell. On the way into detention, I told the arrested male he didn't need to say anything at all. He answered he knew that. I told him that was not what I meant. I meant I did not want to hear his voice at all except when he was getting booked in. He could call a lawyer and then get to a cell, which was probably the safest place for him right about then. After he was booked in, he declined to call a lawyer and went back to his cell without a word. It was probably the only smart thing he did that night.

After he was in his cell, the adrenaline began to come out of me and the spray ran into my eyes. We're sprayed with pepper spray as part of our training and it is painful, but nowhere near as painful as the bear spray. It has a higher concentration of irritant and is more granular. You swear a lot because of the pain, but at least I was in the station and not on the street by the time I could not see anymore.

The staff sergeant and the other members of the platoon were helping to decontaminate the three affected officers. Chemical irritants affect different people differently. Some people are immediately incapacitated and have extreme difficulty breathing; others, like me, cough and choke but the effects take longer to take hold, and I was not sprayed directly in the face. My officers' skin was completely red, and they were unable to work for several hours. For some reason, chemical agents like bear spray seem to affect light-haired and blue-eyed people worse than others. The recruit was blue-eyed and blonde-haired, so she was in the hurt locker.

They all did pretty well given the circumstances. The suspect was arrested on his parole warrant and charged with three counts of assaulting a police officer with a weapon.

What had happened when the officers initially arrived at the call? The suspect fled down the side of the house and went right back in the back door. He tried to lock himself in the bathroom, and when the officers tried to get into the bathroom to arrest him, he unloaded the whole can of bear spray into their faces. He pleaded guilty and was sentenced to an additional six months on top of the time he had yet to serve on his parole violation.

Incidents where officers are hurt are also incidents where there is the highest probability of police overreaction. It's natural to want a bit of payback for the offender. This is where supervision in the field is most important. Not to say my officers would have punched him out or anything (although I know I truly wanted to). By taking control of the situation and taking custody of the offender, I hope I set an example for the officers they will remember when it's their turn to lead.

Lack of supervision on the street has cost many police services enormously. Officers have been jailed and many more have lost their jobs due to a lack of supervision in the field. If patrol sergeants do not get out onto the streets, there is always a possibility that the officers on the street will think they can do whatever they want. They can start to take shortcuts, or they can take an extra shot when someone resists arrest.

The current Saskatoon Police Service is equipped with in-car cameras and GPS in all cars, but sometimes I think we can rely too much on technology to ensure integrity. There will always be a place for a field supervisor. There will always be a need for leadership. There is no substitute for boots on the ground when something happens.

8.

Cheap and Destructive Highs

In the late 1980s, Saskatoon had a solvent abuse problem. Lacquer thinner, cheap and accessible, was the drug of choice among the poorest of the poor. The users were predominantly youths, ten to twenty-five years of age, and almost all native.

They would have sniffing parties. The act of getting high was simple. They took some lacquer thinner and poured it on some cloth, or a "soak" as it was called. They held it to their mouth and nose, and inhaled the noxious fumes. They became enveloped in a cloud, their peripheral vision was reduced, and they were free. Free from poverty, free from broken homes, free from sexual abuse and whatever else ailed them.

The sniffers stole cars and committed incredibly violent acts. Children as young as ten were being pulled from stolen cars. It was out of control. It was also predominately an Indian problem, attracting little official attention. Police reacted, arrested, and processed, and nothing else was getting done.

When I went to calls—and there were a lot of calls involving sniffers—I was instantly angry. I hated the smell, and any contact guaranteed a headache. The sniffers would be glassy-eyed and so intent on their high you would have to knock the soaks out of their hands to get them to stop.

It seemed that the detectives were not interested in dealing with this, and as far as I could tell, our administration couldn't have cared less. In the police world, it was my experience that the most vocal people in the community received the most attention. Native kids sniffing solvents was certainly not a headline grabber, and while tragic, it doesn't grip the imagination of the general public. To me, it was a horrendous form of addiction that affected many people, and something needed to be done.

I started to interview these kids after they were arrested. Where were they getting lacquer thinner? What were the effects?

They were poor, and some of their parents were dysfunctional. There were even multigenerational families getting high together. When they were high, their peripheral vision narrowed significantly, which made them paranoid, explaining why they were so violent.

They were all ashamed of their addiction. One boy was so ashamed, he hung himself. The detective sergeant who came to the call told me that because I was native and knew the family, he thought it would be better if I notified the family of the death. I'd interviewed the boy two weeks prior. I knew his mother, a good woman who did everything she could to help break his addiction to the solvents. The boy hung himself from a tree.

I went to the mother's address. A neighbour told me she was in the park behind the apartments where she lived, having a picnic with her other children. I went there, parked my patrol car, and got out. I could see her with her other children, smiling and laughing. She yelled hello and waved to me. I do not know what face I had on, but she knew instantly why I was there. She began to yell, "No, no, no," and ran away from me. I hated my job right then. I ran after her, tackling her down and telling her that her son was dead. She slapped me and held me tight. A mother's grief is so raw, so emotional, and so utterly draining. I was exhausted.

I told her what I knew and left knowing she would never see me again without reliving the anguish of this day.

My interviews with the solvent abusers revealed a pattern. Adults were providing the lacquer thinner to these kids. Adults with the means bought gallon cans and broke it down into glass juice containers and sold these to the kids. Kids who could not afford to pay for it would be sexually exploited. There was no law to prevent trafficking of lacquer thinner. The kids were not talking about the sex because they needed the lacquer.

I had identified the main perpetrator as a native male in his forties. He was the Pied Piper of the sniffing scene. A big man, 240-plus pounds, he wore his hair in a long braid and almost always wore a Billy Jack–type hat. His face was scarred from a previous attempt to shoot himself. He probably had a story as tragic as his victims, but instead he turned predator. He became my public enemy number one.

I went to the *Criminal Code* and read and reread sections involving negligence and bodily harm, determined to bring him to account. Finally, I found the section that seemed applicable. It was section 180, common nuisance; basically anyone who creates a situation endangering the lives, safety, or health of the public creates a common nuisance. It was time to act.

A reporter was doing a story on solvent abuse for the CBC. I took her and a cameraman on a ride-along out onto the streets to let them see for themselves. It was well-rounded piece, which ended with the doctor talking about the catastrophic effect of lacquer abuse on the body. I am sure a few shook their heads, but it garnered little feedback. I did not hear anything from our administration.

I drafted a search warrant and had it duly sworn. I did not ask anyone to help, nor did anyone offer. Sniffing was the least glamorous and most physically difficult abuse to deal with. Constables were supportive in a kind of "Are you really going to do this?" way. They did come with me when I went to do the search. The warrant specified the items we were looking for: large cans of lacquer thinner, small jars of lacquer thinner, and any related evidence.

We got to the large, second-floor apartment and were met by my suspect. I arrested and handcuffed him. There were several youths in the residence, all high and disoriented. Logistically, it was nightmare, especially because it seemed nobody truly cared at the time. We managed to get everybody sorted out, either arrested or transported home, and we began our search. There was more than enough evidence to support the charge. My suspect was providing solvents to the youths from big cans of lacquer thinner broken down into juice bottles.

As I escorted him out, we had to descend a long staircase. He started to struggle and to resist.

The story could have ended right then. My suspect personified evil. But he made it to the station in good order. I left my reports. The detention corporal said he had never heard of this charge before and he was reluctant to lodge my suspect. More arguments and explaining ensued, and the suspect was placed in cells. I got the attitude "You will step in," and "I can't wait" from more than a few officers when doing things out of the norm. I was pushing the envelope, and sometimes some officers got nervous when I tried new ways to adapt and apply the current laws, such as they were, to new and emerging problems.

My suspect pleaded guilty and received a one-year sentence. God bless the judge and the Crown because I had no idea what would happen in court.

This sentence gave me time to interview the youths, male and female, about my suspicions that he had molested them while they were high and addicted. It was difficult to track them down while they were working through their addictions to solvents and breaking down their misplaced loyalties. My suspect had made them feel they were part of something like a street gang on a much more basic scale. He fed them, kept them high, gave them a place to sleep, and provided clothing.

Eventually, when they were convinced he was in jail and their connection was broken, their families and I got them to co-operate. They provided written statements, but often the statements were sparse and lacked detail, for many of these kids had brain damage as a result of sniffing. It would take years to recover from the effects. Some never did. What they gave me was enough, however, to lay eight sex-related charges against my suspect. I did this without consulting the Crown or my supervisors. At the time, I felt I would have been shut down, either because I was not senior enough or because these cases were too difficult to prosecute.

The methodology of investigating sexual offenses against children has improved 1,000 per cent since I started policing. The changes came as a result of cases where monsters were created and innocent people's lives and reputations were trampled due to hysteria and overzealous investigators looking for the big case. In the late 1980s and early 1990s, for example, there were several cases of wild accusations of satanic child abuse in the United States and even here in Saskatchewan during the Martensville affair, which ultimately fell apart after thorough investigation.

If the current system had been in effect back in the late 1980s, the suspect would probably still be in prison. Well, probably not, but I'd like to think that was possible. As it was, prior to the trials, I received several warnings to watch my back. Perhaps some felt I was making the detectives and administration look bad when all I wanted was to put an end to the solvent problem.

The matter ultimately made it to the Court of Queen's Bench. I served subpoenas to everyone involved. They still had addiction problems and mixed loyalties, and my victims, with the exception of one, regularly did not show up for court. His street name was Hamburger, and when the suspect saw that he was at court, he pleaded guilty to a single count of sexual assault. He received a two-year sentence.

Other officers went on to charge two other males who were providing lacquer thinner to youths with creating a common nuisance based on my case and experience. Within a year, solvent abuse had ceased to be a major problem in the city of Saskatoon.

Hamburger was murdered a year and half later. His killer was a sniffer who had turned to alcohol. The charge was dismissed and ruled as self-defence. The rest of the kids from the circle never truly recovered. One of the girls suffered long-term damage from solvent abuse, causing her to be wheelchair-bound. Another of the girls turned to prostitution and was murdered by the serial killer Mark Crawford. One of the boys would play a significant part in my involvement with the Stonechild Inquiry.

When I first started with the Saskatoon Police Force, the poorest people and the hardest of the hard-core alcoholics drank Lysol, a common housecleaning disinfectant. Lysol was cheap and readily available. They would puncture the cans and mix the contents with water to get an extremely strong, high-alcohol-content drink. Its smell was distinctive, and the level of intoxication was extreme.

Shocking as it seems that people would subject their bodies to this type of abuse, it did not surprise me. I had seen later-stage alcoholics in Northern Ontario drink vanilla extract for its alcohol content. Even the consumption of aftershave lotion was not unheard of. It just seemed to be a sad and unfortunate part of life back then.

The situation was different now. I was police officer. I could do something about it.

By October 1989, I had had enough of picking up drunks intoxicated with Lysol. To me, the legal and social costs seemed enormous. It was a quality-of-life issue to the people of the neighbourhood. The fact that it went on day after day reflected poorly on our police service.

I started by interviewing two people I dealt with who were drinking Lysol, and they identified where they had purchased it. There was a small confectionery in the centre of my district that seemed to be the main supplier to the Lysol-drinking crowd. The prices would vary. The highest price was charged when welfare cheques came out. The price would drop in the days before cheque day.

The confectionery had been subject of Crime Stoppers tips, and a detective sergeant had attempted an undercover purchase of Lysol in 1987. Unfortunately, his investigation did not lead to any charges. Senior officers actively discouraged me when I broached the idea of going after the owner of the confectionery for knowingly selling Lysol as an alcoholic beverage—it had been tried before without success and they thought I was wasting my time.

I checked *The Alcohol Control Act* and found two sections I believed the confectionery owner and his staff were knowingly violating. It was an offence under *The Alcohol Control Act* to sell a compound containing alcohol for the purposes of producing an alcoholic beverage. I got a search warrant, and two constables and I went to the confectionery to execute it. The employee on duty immediately called the owner. On the wall behind the counter, there was a crude handwritten sign that said "Not for human consumption." Behind the counter were two open cases of Lysol nearly empty. Seven full cases were found by the back door. The confectionery was small, no larger than the size of a living room. The cash register tape showed that in a two-day period, this shoebox-sized confectionery had sold thirteen cases of Lysol at six dollars a can, with twelve cans to a case.

The owner of the confectionery showed up and was given a copy of the search warrant. He immediately called a lawyer. He stated that he didn't know people were drinking Lysol. His contempt for me and the investigation were readily apparent. He asked me why I cared. His true nature came out when he added that he couldn't help it if the Indians wanted it, and his lawyer said it was perfectly fine for him to sell this Lysol. He told me I was smartass cop, and I would get what was coming to me.

He struck me as a cold and cruel man. Lysol is 80 to 85 per cent ethanol alcohol and devastating to the human body. He just didn't care. I issued him a receipt for the seized product, and we left.

I had earlier spoken to a delivery driver who was delivering to the confectionery and had identified the company where the Lysol had been purchased. A week after we executed the search warrant, I went there and spoke with an employee in charge of accounts receivable and credit. I asked for the records showing how much Lysol had been delivered to the confectionery for the period January 1989 until the time of the search warrant. The employee said she would gladly do this, as the sale of Lysol to this confectionery had been the subject of concern to her and her company in general.

The records showed that the owner of the confectionery had purchased 228 cases of Lysol, amounting to 2,836 cans of Lysol at an average wholesale price of $3.11 a can during that period. It did not count cases of Lysol purchased at the cash and carry. Using an average retail price of $6.00 per can, it showed almost $17,000 in sales and $8,000 in profit. Not bad for a confectionery the size of a shoebox! It sold more Lysol than any other store in the city of Saskatoon, including major grocers.

The case was flawed. I had only one witness who was willing to testify. The witness had direct knowledge of the accused knowingly selling Lysol for consumption, but he was assaulted prior to the trial date and then refused to co-operate. The Crown was not willing to proceed without a witness. The charge was stayed.

The accused, however, stopped selling Lysol as the local media was all over him. He had been exposed. It wasn't the outcome I wanted, but it was a good outcome nonetheless.

A couple of months later, I went to assist paramedics dealing with a person who had had a heart attack. While at the call, I saw numerous bottles of Chinese cooking wine. The victim had been drinking it with her friends.

I went to St Paul's Hospital and spoke to the emergency room doctor, who explained that Chinese cooking wine has a high alcohol content, but it also has a high salt content, enough to spike the blood pressure, causing heart attacks when consumed as liquor.

Once again, the most vulnerable people are at risk. It would be easy to wash your hands of it all. These people were making their own choices, and if it were not Chinese cooking wine, it would be something else. True enough on its face.

The offence comes when people see a vulnerable and exploitable segment of society and then facilitates the addiction for their own personal gain. They are like whiskey traders of old. Their contempt for the people consuming Chinese cooking wine cleared their conscience.

I had learned from the Lysol case what I needed to get the charges to put an end to this. Every person I caught drinking Chinese cooking wine I charged and interviewed. A lot of them were ashamed of their addiction and hated how sick the wine made them. Almost all of them had friends who had been hospitalized, and a couple had friends who had died consuming the wine.

This time, my investigation did not make other patrol officers impatient with the fact that I wasn't taking as many calls as they were. After the Lysol consumption had dried up, they were happy to let me tackle this problem.

Over the course of my investigation, I learned that a Vietnamese specialty store in the heart of Riversdale was the main source of Chinese cooking wine. So as not to interfere with the legitimate business in the front, the store-owners' method of operation was to have the alcoholics come to the back door to purchase the wine, which was then wrapped in newspaper and put in a plastic bag. They were then told to leave out the back alley and to avoid the police.

Once again, the price of the wine varied in accordance with the welfare cheque days. The cooking wine, in spite of its high alcohol content, was not regulated or subject to the high taxes of legal alcohol products. My suspects were making 100 to 150 per cent profit on each bottle they sold. They taught the alcoholics to ask for the wine by the name of *muka-hi. Mukahi,* I learned, is a terrible insult in Chinese, so if the people who drank the wine went into any other store and asked for it, they would have been promptly thrown out. My suspects had the market cornered.

I started to do surveillance in a marked patrol car and started picking people up as they came out the back door of the store. I stopped one vehicle driven by a white male that had five native persons in it after it left the rear of the store. The driver gave me a statement indicating that he was paid regularly by these people to drive them to the store so they could buy the wine.

I got a search warrant. Three constables and I went to execute it. The store manager was served with the warrant. He indicated that he didn't speak English. There was no wine displayed on any counter or shelf. We did find twenty-eight cases, with twenty-four bottles of cooking wine to a case, in the storeroom by the back door. Beside the cases were piles of newspapers and plastic bags. While we were conducting the search, several people came to the back door looking to purchase the wine.

We seized what records we could. The records were all in either Vietnamese or Chinese. Just from the numbers on the invoices, it appeared that the store had sold 366 cases of cooking wine between March and July 1990. It was a lot of misery to spread around.

Prior to the trial—and I wanted a trial so we could make case law—I received subpoenas for the store staff, all of whom were family members of the owner. I served them, all the while receiving a barrage of curses. The lawyer for the accused tried to have the subpoenas quashed as they were served on the staff on short notice. The judge refused and ordered the staff to attend court. The accused pleaded guilty and received a six-hundred-dollar fine. The local media covered it all, and the cooking wine problem was done.

Since this case, other types of denatured alcohol have surfaced. Mouthwash and hairspray are commonly consumed. No one store has been the central seller. The alcoholics search for different stores so as not to lose their source.

There was a human rights decision in Regina where a male succeeded in a complaint against a major retailer who would not sell him mouthwash. I just shook my head. Alternate alcohol is still a problem. It's just not as rampant as it used to be. Now, as a sergeant, I tell my officers to deal with problems that affect the community and the quality of life as a priority. These are stories I use to hammer home the point. Do something.

Explaining why you are there goes a long way. (Courtesy Saskatoon Police Service)

9.

One Strong Woman

Women are the victims of some of the most horrible crimes, and historically, native women in Canada have endured more than their share. Once again, where I had chosen to work ensured I would be witness to some of those crimes.

In 1991, a constable was at St Paul's Hospital checking on the injuries of young child who had been struck by a car. He was approached by an emergency room doctor, who told him that a woman had been seriously assaulted but did not want any police involvement. The constable went to speak with her in spite of what she had told the doctor. The victim's injuries were obvious and extensive. She told the constable who was responsible and how scared she was of him. The victim told the constable she was going to leave the province. The officer could not persuade the woman to pursue charges. He left a report for informational purposes and requested that a copy go to the Morality section. He listed the responsible male as a suspect. The report was dictated at 1800 hours, or 6 p.m., on 21 April.

About the time the report was being left, I started shift. At the time, I was assigned to the beat with a senior constable. The suspect in the assault was wanted on a Canada-wide warrant for breach of parole. We knew nothing about the report the constable had left. After the bars closed, we got a car and started looking for the parole violator. We went to a likely address, and as we were getting ready to check the house for the fugitive, a woman approached us. I knew her from walking the beat. She told me her friend had been badly beaten and asked if we would talk to her.

We went into the residence and I met the victim in the kitchen. She was a small woman. Her face was swollen and covered with bruises and cuts. Her left eye was completely swollen shut. Her arms were deeply bruised and she had stitches on one arm. Even her own mother would not have recognized her. At first she was frantic, panicking, because her friend had brought the police there. She adamantly insisted that she just wanted to leave the province with her children. The woman had been cowed into submission and believed the threats the suspect had made against her. I spent the next hour and a half talking to her, first trying to gain her trust and empowering her to see the charges through. The tipping point came when I asked her what she would tell her daughter to do if her daughter were in front of her and in the condition she was in. Her body language was a mix of relief and fear as she came to the patrol car to be taken to the station for a statement and have her injuries photographed.

This emotionally and physically battered, exhausted woman provided a detailed witness statement over the course of the next three hours. Her story was horrifying. She had been in a relationship with the suspect for about five months. I knew the suspect to be a very active criminal in the downtown crime scene, involved with guns, drugs, and prostitution, and I was puzzled why this soft-spoken woman would have been with him in the first place. She had begun to hear stories about him and to doubt how committed and sincere he was about the relationship. On the night before her ordeal began, she had slept with another man after a night of drinking. She was struggling and had made up her mind to get out of the unhealthy relationship she had with the suspect.

On 20 April, the suspect called her and said he wanted to work things out. She drove her car with her children in car seats to pick him up. They drove to her home and parked. He pressed her into admitting that she had slept with another man and then punched her in the face two or three times, bloodying her face. All the while, her children were asleep in their car seats. The argument continued until the suspect demanded oral sex. He was calling her a whore and a pig all the while. She complied, and he left after a patrol car passed by. He had an outstanding warrant for his arrest, and he knew it. He told her that he would be back the next day.

He came by cab the evening of the 21st at around 8 p.m. with his fifteen-year-old son. The victim's children were in bed. He immediately started in on her, telling his son that she was a whore, and began punching her repeatedly in the face. She begged for forgiveness. He told her that she meant nothing to him and that he was going to hurt her. He ordered her into the bedroom; she pleaded with him to stop, but went. He told her to get on the bed while he grabbed a hammer out of the closet. He hit her on the arms and told her to stop crying or he would use it on her head. She begged him to stop, saying that she had had enough. He told her she had not had anything yet, and she was a piece of shit whore who deserved to die. The suspect told her he was going to cut her up and mark her for life. He looked around for something sharp and not finding anything, started punching the swollen part of her face. He grabbed the hammer and told her to put her knees over the bed so he could smash her kneecaps.

As I sat writing her statement, I watched her: exhausted, ashamed, and now relieved to tell her story. It was like walking on eggshells—one wrong word, one wrong look, and she would shut it down, go back to being a passive victim, and forgive this man who had inflicted such suffering. Another deep breath and a shudder and she continued.

He hit her with a bar while she was on the bed, forcing her to keep her arms to the side so she could not defend herself. At one point, he told her to come out of the bedroom and to wash the blood off of her face. They sat in the kitchen. He settled down and asked her to sit in his lap. He kissed her face, told her he loved her and apologized for messing up her face. The suspect maintained his control over her by saying he had to take his son somewhere to explain what had happened. She promised not to leave the house. He was sober all through this, and the victim thought the worst was over. The suspect left with his son at about 10:30 p.m. He returned with his son around 2:30 a.m. His son was carrying beer in a grocery bag. The suspect had an open beer in his hand. The victim knew he was high on pills as well. He questioned her to ensure that she had not called her friend or said anything to anybody about the beating she had endured. Once he had established that she had not told anyone, he said that was a good thing because he wanted to kill her, and if she had told anyone, there would have been evidence against him. He took three Fiornal and told her to wait until they kicked in.

I knew Fiornal as a street drug known as fire, with effects similar to PCP. People on Fiornal are violent. My victim must have known what was coming. The suspect told the victim she was going to be tortured and then killed. She begged and pleaded with him, telling him that she had two small children. All the while, he was punching the injured part of her face. He told his son to get a knife from the kitchen, but he refused. The victim asked the son to run and get help. He did not. The suspect then broke a beer bottle and with the jagged edge sliced her arm. He then broke a bottle on her head. The suspect became even more enraged when glass got on his hands. He ordered her into the bathroom and made her stand in the tub to clean off the blood. Her blood splattered on his white shirt. He became incensed at this and grabbed the hammer. He went to swing it at her as she crouched in the tub with the water running and she blocked it with her arm, which caused it to ricochet and hit him under the eye, cutting him. He told her she would pay dearly for making him bleed, and at some point he urinated on her while she was in the tub.

He ordered her to into the bedroom and told her to lie on the bed. He kept hitting her and ordered her to keep her arms to the side and not to touch him because she was a filthy bitch. He broke two more beer bottles over her head. He made her lie on her hands and alternated punching her face and ribs. He was smoking and flicking ashes at her face. He then told her to lie still, and he lay down beside her. She told him she did not want to have sex, and that reignited his fury. He told her to get up and get the Vaseline. She said no but finally did. She tried to refuse him, to no avail, and he took her anally. When he thought she was not enjoying it enough, he took his penis out of her and stuck it in her swollen mouth, asking her if she liked the taste of her own feces.

I kept writing. One wrong word, one wrong look, and this evidence would be gone.

The suspect ordered the by now thoroughly humiliated woman to get a bread bag and put it on his penis. He made her mount him and jump up and down, punching her in the face while she was doing it and calling her a pig. She got off of him and tried to hide in the corner of the bedroom. He punched her several more times, spit in her face, and threatened to shove the rod he had used earlier to beat her inside her. He dragged her into the living room and made her sit on the floor beside him, telling her it was because she was a dog. He kicked her in the face whenever she tried to hide her face. The suspect then asked her to sit in his lap and told her no one would want her now. He told her he should have killed her.

I looked up. She was done. I had her sign her statement and without comment took her to the forensic corporal, who photographed her numerous injuries. My partner and I then drove her to her friend's house to wait for her mother, who was coming in from out of the province to take her home. The victim's children were there and safe. She provided us with the keys to her home.

By now, dawn was breaking. All the evidence the victim described was there: broken beer bottles, the rod, a bloody facecloth, and blood in every room. There was what appeared to be urine on the tub and the bathroom floor. We secured the residence until the day shift forensic officer came on and then seized everything. I exhibited it all and left my report and requested warrants for the suspect.

A long, emotional night ended about two seconds after my head hit the pillow. The victim's long and horrible ordeal lay front and centre in my thoughts.

The suspect was arrested a couple of days later. There had been a murder in a downtown bar, and it was believed he was involved. The emergency response team took him into custody. When photographed, the suspect had a small cut under his left eye exactly where the victim had said the hammer had hit him. He was remanded to await his trial. He was never charged with murder, so the parole violation and the charges I laid were the ones that kept him in jail.

At the preliminary hearing, the victim did well testifying about the assaults, however she downplayed the sexual offences. He was committed to stand trial at the Court of Queen's Bench. I enlisted the help of the RCMP in the province where the victim was living to keep her on track. The crown prosecutor was totally committed to this case. She worked long and hard to ensure that the suspect would be convicted in spite of the reluctance of the victim to fully co-operate.

She was a classic battered woman. She still believed she could help him and change him. She somehow believed it was her fault that all of this had happened to her.

The trial was set for November 1991, and I was more than prepared to testify. Just prior to the trial, the accused and his lawyer offered a plea bargain to avoid the suspect being branded as a sex offender in prison. He pleaded guilty to three charges—assault, assault with a weapon, and assault causing bodily harm—and received a three-year sentence in a federal penitentiary.

At his sentencing, the suspect did everything he could to minimize the violence and sexual offences he had committed. He had no insight into the horror and pain he had inflicted on this woman. His defence lawyer argued that because the children did not wake up, the children's presence was not an aggravating factor, but I never believed the children had slept through the victim's entire ordeal. The suspect was asked if he had anything to say before the sentence was passed. He said he still loved her and cared for her. The judge could barely control his anger and could hardly hide his contempt as he sarcastically asked the suspect if this was how he showed his love.

I never saw the victim again. I do not know where she is or what she is doing. I have never seen the convicted man. As far as I know, he still lives in Saskatoon, but I never dealt with him again. The dedicated crown prosecutor who ran this difficult case is now the head of public prosecutions in the city of Saskatoon. I stayed in Patrol.

Several years later, my partner and I were having a busy night shift. We raced from call to call, making arrests and living off caffeine and adrenaline. A call came in: a woman was beaten and naked behind a local Tim Horton's. I knew the night staff, a friendly older woman who loved her community. When we arrived, she had wrapped a blanket around the badly beaten and completely naked woman. The victim blurted out the story of what had happened to her, and we called for an ambulance. She had met a man while walking who started up a conversation with her. As they were walking and talking, they passed a parking lot, and there he attacked her. She fought back hard, scratching and biting. He raped her and beat her with a board that had nails sticking out of it. She kept fighting until she was able to run. She was a strong woman.

She went off with the ambulance. My partner and I split the investigation. He would handle the crime scene and the search for the suspect. I would go to the hospital to get more information and a statement.

Before we split up, we went to the staff sergeant and briefed him. We had a good description. Our victim was sure that she had scratched his face, and we wanted him to do a press release with the description and the additional detail of the scratched face. He told us it was out of the ordinary to do press releases on these types of crimes. We politely insisted, and he did it.

I did about six hours of overtime taking a detailed statement from our victim and making arrangements to ensure she was cared for. She was such a strong woman. I was filled with admiration for her.

I went home to catch a few hours of sleep before returning for our last night shift. When I got to work, the suspect was in custody. The description released to the public was the key. The director of the local Indian and Métis Friendship Centre saw a male with scratches on his face, knew his name, and called police. The Community Response unit members, bicycle-mounted patrol officers, got him on the trails down by the river. It turned out that he had just been released from the penitentiary for a violent sexual assault on a chambermaid at a hotel in another Saskatchewan city.

My partner and I were elated. The crown prosecutor assigned to the case received a call from another woman who had heard the press coverage and suspected that she had been attacked by the same man. The crown prosecutor called me and asked if I would interview her. What a change from my early years in Saskatoon! This is the way we should always have worked together. The woman gave a detailed statement. Her ordeal was as harrowing as the first woman's, except she was smaller and less able to fight the man off.

I laid more charges, and with the help of the crown prosecutor's office, I obtained a DNA warrant. My suspect, a native man, would have attacked me at the drop of a hat given the opportunity as we took his blood. His hatred burned with searing intensity as he stared at me. The purest of predators, he was an evil man. I cannot help but think of the pain and terror he had inflicted on his victims.

The DNA came back a match. The witnesses testified and the suspect was convicted. The crown prosecutor made an application to have the convicted man declared a dangerous sex offender, effectively taking him off the streets forever. He was declared a dangerous offender after a hearing. His only words when asked to speak were "Fuck you, man," and he was led away, struggling with the RCMP officers who were taking him to the penitentiary.

There's no better feeling than when everything goes right. Victims stand up for themselves and testify. Members of the public call the police. The crown and the police work together. The linchpin, of course, is the victim. These women were so strong, and if it were not so "private" a crime, I would have loved to have them talk to other victims. Your voice is strong when you have been victimized, and we need your voice.

No detectives were involved in any of these cases. Nobody came forward to offer advice or help. I do not know if it was like that for everyone back then, but for me, the fleet seemed to remain at anchor. The crown prosecutors were excellent. On the case of a dangerous offender, the crown prosecutor helped me to draw up the warrant for the suspect's DNA, which was a fairly new procedure at the time.

In the present Saskatoon Police Service, plainclothes investigators would be assigned to assist or lead the investigation. Investigations have become more complex and the courts have come to expect more from the police. The courts have criticized the police for not recording victim statements electronically. Everything takes more time now, but things are done to a higher standard. Sometimes I wonder whether, if we had had the same level of co-operation and professionalism we have now from the day I started, I would have had some very different stories to tell.

10.

Semper vigilans — Assume Nothing

I had less than a year with the Saskatoon Police Department when I was sent to a domestic involving two senior citizens. The dispatcher said there was no backup available, but I assumed that because of their ages, I would be fine. I pulled up several houses away and walked up to a small wartime house. Yellow with white trim, adorned with old-fashioned curtains, and surrounded by a white picket fence with a well-worn gate, it looked like the respectable home of elderly people. The yard was clean and neat. There was a large garden in the back, well laid out and weed free.

I went to the porch and glanced inside. I saw a female at the kitchen table. She appeared to be crying. I knocked quietly and opened the door. The house smelled of liniment and strong coffee. The woman, in her seventies, stopped crying and looked up. I asked her what was going on, keeping my eye on a closed bedroom door. In a trembling voice, she explained that her husband, who was eighty-eight years old, was being mean to her. I asked where he was, and she pointed to a bedroom door.

I was being complacent, lulled by their ages and the quaintness of their little home. I was going to give the old fellow a good talking to and be cleared of this call for something more exciting. I went to the bedroom door. It was heavy and solid, covered with many coats of paint and keyed with an old-fashioned key lock. I pushed it open gently and saw her husband curled up in bed, apparently asleep. He wore suspenders, a long-sleeved shirt, green work pants, and wool socks, even though it was summer.

I turned and went back to the woman to tell her that her husband was asleep and have her expand on what her husband was doing to be mean to her. I was not thinking anything criminal had occurred. I got my notebook out and began to write down her particulars when I felt a hard poke in the small of my back. I heard the distinctive sound of the trigger being pulled on an empty chamber. I turned quickly and saw that my harmless old man was not harmless at all. He had a rifle in his hand and had fully intended to shoot me. He wasn't a little man either—he was six feet tall and strong. I wrestled the gun from him and tried to handcuff him without hurting him. He must have done manual labour his whole life because it took everything I had to twist him into handcuffs.

The woman was crying again. I was not going to make the same mistake again—I didn't turn my back to her. I called for backup, and another other young constable showed up. I explained what had happened and asked him to call Social Services or see if he could find any family members to take care of the woman. I took the husband to my patrol car and secured him inside. I then checked the rifle. The safety was off and there was a loaded magazine in it. He had not racked a round into the chamber. If he had, I would have been crippled or dead.

It turned out that my guy was a retired farmer, married for fifty-plus years, and he had the onset of Alzheimer's. He refused to take any medical advice or treatment. He was stubborn and prideful. His family and his wife could not handle him anymore.

I charged him with attempted murder and clearly stated in my report that if he were ordered by the courts to get treatment, I would be satisfied with that remedy.

I got some stupid and sarcastic comments from other police officers as I was booking the old fellow in. Until I told the story—then it was not funny anymore.

My youngest son had just started wrestling, and like all novices, he was losing most of his matches, when he said to me, "Dad, what do you know about fighting?"

I started to give him some advice, but before I could say anything, my wife held up her hand and said, "I got this one."

Every police officer who is on the street will eventually be assaulted. Every officer on the street will at some time have to use physical force to effect an arrest. Police officers do their best to avoid this, but sometimes you just cannot.

Losing a physical confrontation is not an option when you are the police. Physical fitness, training, and mental preparation should not be an option either. It's your responsibility and duty to be fit and mentally prepared. Your own and someone else's life could depend on it. It sounds dramatic, but it is the truth.

I've been spit at many times, and head-butted, but only once. I have been punched, kicked, and bitten. I have punched, kicked, and choked out people. I have pepper sprayed arrests and struck them with batons, both the old wooden and new metal ones.

The common denominator in most of these incidents is they happened when I least expected them to. Persons determined to escape or hurt you don't carry a sign saying that's what they're going to do, but instinct and experience will give you some warning, and you need to trust in them. A person who's going to fight you because you are a police officer does not care who you are. They don't care that you have a family. They don't know or care if you are having a good day or bad day.

Over the years, you learn to play smarter. You try not to go into bars alone, realizing that it is possible to step back and wait until other officers get there. But there were times when you just could not.

I'm not telling these stories to show how tough I am. Experienced yes, but tough no. I'm telling them to emphasize physical and mental preparedness. If you're a police officer or are thinking of being a police officer, you need to keep in mind that things can happen quickly, and you must be prepared.

There such a balancing act for police officers when they are on the street. There is sometimes a need to be utterly ruthless, to win the fight with whatever means you have. It cannot be helped—for example, when you tackle someone fleeing from a violent crime. It is violence, fast and furious—tempered, but violence nonetheless. How do you keep the edge and be prepared for murderous, horrific people and still keep your humanity?

All people—or almost all people—have aspirations and want to live peacefully. Some, due to circumstances, cannot, and they end up coming in conflict with the laws of the land. If you accept the premise that most people are good at heart, you as a police officer can navigate this complex and difficult world. But when the time comes, you are still a warrior charged with the protection of those who are not. You have to mix friendly and approachable with just enough attitude to look a little dangerous.

There is an old saying in the army, "Hard in training, easy in war." It's not exactly true but it is true enough. The Saskatoon Police Service has improved its training in all aspects of self-defence. From shooting to ground fighting, the officers we have been hiring are better trained than I was. Tactically, they operate smarter. But there is no substitute for shared experience, and every story I tell can be looked at several ways: What did we learn? How can we prevent something like that from happening again? Is there a better way? Almost always there will be a better way, and you can always learn something.

Will any police service ever be able to prevent sudden and violent assaults on police officers? No, unfortunately it is part of being a police officer. You accept the inevitable and try to be prepared.

Around 1996, another constable and I received information that a break-and-enter suspect was at his father's home. There was an outstanding warrant for the suspect's arrest. His father was a decent man who was frustrated with his son's criminal activity and wanted it to end, even if it meant that his son went to jail.

We parked half a block away and crept up to the house. I knocked quietly on the door, and the father answered. He did not say anything but pointed to a bedroom door. He motioned that his son would run. We quietly approached the door. I gently turned the knob and pushed. It was blocked. I motioned to the other constable that I was going to kick it, and we got ready. I lifted my foot and kicked the door open, quickly acquiring the suspect's location on a mattress on the floor.

Suddenly, something hit me in the eye, hard. I thought I had been shot, and I drew my revolver while falling backwards. I remember thinking, "No one shoots me for free," and I got my gun on the suspect with my good eye. I had my finger on the trigger and was prepared to fire when a butter knife hit my thigh. The kid's eyes were wide with terror when I realized what had happened. The suspect had used a butter knife to secure the door. When I kicked the door, the frame did not break, rather it bent the knife until the door cleared it. The knife sprang out and whirled through the air until it struck me in the right eye, blade first. The knife cut the white part of my eye and the eyelids, top and bottom.

I holstered my gun, glad I had not shot the suspect.

Growing up in Northern Ontario, it was not uncommon to put a knife in the door when the door did not have a lock. Where I grew up, there were no hardware stores to buy locks at, and we made do. This knowledge saved the young man's life.

He did not say a word as I handcuffed him and told him he was under arrest. The other constable was looking at me, and from his expression, I knew I was hurt.

After the suspect was handcuffed and secure, the adrenaline start to subside, and I noticed blood dripping onto my uniform shirt, boots, and the bedroom floor. It must have been a sight for the suspect: two police officers kicking down his door, one hurt and angry, the other as shocked as the suspect. I found a mirror, took one look, turned over the arrest to the other constable, and drove myself to St Paul's Hospital. A nurse fast-tracked me to an area just off the emergency room. The attending doctor, whom I knew from many years of contacts, came in and cleaned me up. Cleaned up, I looked like hell. He made quick phone call and told me that one of the top eye specialists in the city would be free for an hour and he would see me. I thanked him, grabbed a pair of the safety goggles the paramedics wear, and raced to the downtown office of the specialist.

I got to the specialist's office and was getting booked in when I realized I did not have my health card. I do not call my wife very much, on purpose because I do not want her to worry, but now I had to call. I nonchalantly asked for my health card number. My wife would have been a good detective or lawyer. She pressed me until I gave up and told her what had happened.

The doctor told me I was not going to lose my eye and gave me powerful eye drops to help the healing. I worked the rest of the shift with my mangled eye and the goggles and was happy when it was over so I could go home. I was telling the story when my beautiful little daughter came over and, with the directness of a child, promptly stuck her finger in my injured eye while asking, "Daddy, what happened to your eye?"

I do not know what happened to the arrest. I did not even check. The eye healed, and except for a film from the scar tissue in one part of my vision, there was no permanent damage.

What struck me most about this whole incident was the goodwill of the hospital staff, the nurses and doctors who went out of their way to ensure I received first-rate treatment, and that I got it quickly. To any police officer, the benefits of working in an area until everyone knows you should be obvious.

Sunday morning, a day shift in April 1997, started off as most Sunday day shifts do, quiet and uneventful. A call came in from a young woman who alleged that she had been held captive and sexually assaulted by her aunt and uncle overnight. She told us how she had gone over to visit, and after a few beers the couple had tried to initiate sex. When she refused, they overpowered her and sexually assaulted her. Her aunt was an active participant. At one point they used a bingo dabber as a dildo.

We got her medical attention. She was mentally and physically exhausted. After getting a statement, my partner and I went to arrest the suspects. Both of them were intravenous drug users, and I knew them from previous dealings. The male suspect was a violent career criminal with a long string of convictions.

The female who opened the door when we knocked was obviously not expecting the police. As soon as she realized it was the police, she yelled and tried to slam the door in our faces. As there was evidence that could easily have been destroyed, there was no time to get a warrant until the suspects were custody. We forced our way in. My partner took care of the female and I went in after the male.

He looked wild, high and desperate. He moved to get to a bed, where I later found a large hunting knife. I grabbed his arm and the fight was on. He was high on morphine, so he had a very high tolerance for pain. Control holds were not doing anything, and the arrest just became a fight. The other constable called for backup, and a sergeant arrived while the male and I were still fighting. I got him into a headlock, and we crashed through a glass coffee table, cutting my wrist. The sergeant took custody of the female, and the other constable came in and struck the male with his baton. It did not faze the suspect at all. It was not until a third officer came in that we were able to overpower the suspect and force him into handcuffs. Drenched in sweat and defiant, he was pulled, dragged, and carried out of the apartment to a waiting patrol car. I was already feeling the strain of our prolonged struggle, so I knew that when he came down from his high, he would be hurting and stiff.

Once both of the accused were custody, I cleaned my cut wrist and went to obtain a search warrant for the items described by the victim. All physical evidence the victim said would be there was located and seized. I found the knife the victim told me had been brandished at her to secure her compliance. I found her clothes and the bingo dabber. The bingo dabber still had blood on it. The aunt had had the presence of mind to toss it downstairs onto a pile of laundry while she was fighting with the police.

The male suspect pleaded guilty at his first court appearance and was sentenced to five years in the penitentiary. My cut wrist got infected, and I got blood poisoning. The female pleaded not guilty and made bail, which she promptly skipped. She was arrested later on the outstanding warrants. She wanted a trial and got it, ultimately being convicted and sentenced to two and a half years in jail. The victim recovered from her ordeal and seems to be doing fine.

I make it a point to tell this story to young constables. Even on a Sunday day shift, you still have to be ready for anything.

Follow-up with a victim of domestic abuse
(courtesy The StarPhoenix)

11.

Sticking My Nose In

One of the nicest compliments I have ever received was not a compliment at all. Staff Sergeant Keith Jarvis was being interviewed prior to the Stonechild Inquiry. During the interview, he was asked for his assessment of me. He stated that I had nothing to do with his investigation, and I just had a bad habit of sticking my nose into other people's files — not just his — because I knew a lot of the native community.

I never wanted to tell a "poor me" story, but there were times in my career where people deliberately tried to cause me trouble. Their reasoning and motives were and still are suspect.

Around 1990, I was walking the beat on a night shift outside of one of the most notorious bars in Saskatoon. I saw vehicle parked and running and approached it. A male was passed out in the driver seat and appeared to be drunk. My partner and I began to bang on the windows. He woke up and looked directly at me. He acknowledged that I was a police officer but refused to open the door. I warned him regarding obstruction. He did not seem to care. The patrol wagon came by, manned by two senior officers. The more senior of the members told us there was nothing we could do and to leave it alone.

I was not about to leave this drunken male in a position where he could put the vehicle in motion and be driving onto our streets. I pried the window and eventually managed to unlock the door. I took the male into custody for obstructing a police officer. At his feet was a shotgun. I seized it and laid a number of firearms charges on him and took him off to jail.

Unbeknownst to me, the senior officer from the patrol wagon who had told me to leave the man in the car alone had left an investigation report saying I had exceeded my authority by making the arrest.

A couple weeks later, I received a court notice. I collected my notes and the shotgun and went to court. When I arrived at court, I saw the senior officer there, and I remember thinking that he had nothing to do with this case. He had even driven away while we were still engaged with the suspect. The crown prosecutor approached me and told me that this officer had gone to the defence lawyer and told him the arrest was unlawfully made. He told the defence lawyer and the Crown he was prepared to testify for the defence. This posed an insurmountable problem for the Crown. The Crown would have to discredit at least one of us, and it made the case unwinnable. I was told the charge would be stayed in light of this development.

I was stunned. What was this constable's motive? And why had he not talked to me the night the arrest had been made? I was mad and took the shotgun and threw it to him. I told him to give the shotgun back to the suspect and maybe he could shoot a police officer with it, and then I left.

A couple months later, I took a report of a street robbery from a tall, gangly, mentally challenged man who said my suspect in the shotgun case had robbed him of his Walkman. A Walkman, for people too young to have ever seen one, is a portable cassette player, the predecessor of MP3s and other portable music systems. My victim did not own a lot of things, and his mother had given him the Walkman. I took a statement from him and began to check the local bars for my suspect. The victim knew him by name. I found him and arrested him shortly afterwards. He still had the Walkman. I charged him with robbery and returned the Walkman to my victim.

Months later, I received the court notice that this matter had been set down in the Court of Queen's Bench for trial. The crown prosecutor was worried that my victim did not possess the intellect to stand up to a vigorous cross-examination by defence. I asked to testify first and told the Crown my victim would be fine. The crown prosecutor led my victim through what had happened, and then it was the turn of the defence. The defence lawyer was beaming, anxious to trip up my victim, and was very condescending to him. He asked my victim how he could be so sure his client was the robber. My victim raised his voice and in his plain and simple speech stated, while pointing at the suspect, that he knew what he knew and no one could change that, and he did not care what some lawyer said, "That was the guy who robbed me, and Ernie got him."

His simple conviction and sincerity were more than the defence lawyer had anticipated. The truth has a certain ring to it in a courtroom, and his client was convicted.

After serving his time, the same guy got of jail and returned to Saskatoon. He and another male beat a guy to death with a baseball bat. They were both charged with murder and subsequently were convicted of manslaughter. I heard he was out on parole and have not seen him since.

My victim still lives in Saskatoon and is homeless since his mother died. Too proud to live in assisted housing, he is a fixture in the parks and downtown area. A gentle, simple giant of a man, he walks around the downtown with everything he owns on his back, wearing a crooked toque and wool socks pulled over the top of his pant legs. I talk to him often, and he has never forgotten that I got his Walkman back for him.

Around the same time, I went to a call where a woman had been stabbed several times in the lower abdomen by a male acquaintance. She provided a witness statement and confirmed the suspect's identification during a photo lineup. A couple of other constables and I located and arrested the suspect shortly afterward. He was charged with aggravated assault. He was a career criminal and wanted to provide information in exchange for the charges being dropped. He went so far as to say that the victim was an Indian bitch who would not testify anyway.

He picked the wrong police officer to tell that to.

Prior to trial, my suspect was released on bail, and a subpoena was served on my victim. I could not believe that the suspect had been released, given his lengthy and violent criminal record. On the trial date, I showed up, and the suspect was in the front row of the gallery, looking confident and relaxed, with a senior constable of the Saskatoon police, out of uniform, seated beside him. This officer told me I had "shit," and that this would be over soon. The crown prosecutor asked me what was going on. I did not really have an answer for her and was as perplexed as she was.

The victim's name was called at the start of the trial. She did not answer to her subpoena to attend court. The accused and the constable smiled at me. The defence lawyer asked for the charges to be dismissed for lack of prosecution. There was a short adjournment, and the Crown asked if I could find the victim again. I was confident I could and told her so. Court recommenced, and the Crown argued for and got an adjournment only after the judge admonished me, saying mistaken identity was a serious issue. Apparently, the senior constable had told the defence lawyer this was a case of mistaken identity. The judge made it clear that if my victim was not there after this adjournment, the case would be dismissed.

My partner and I found the victim going out the door of her apartment and arrested her for failing to attend court as a witness. Her reaction triggered the realization that my victim was not who she had said she was. She had lied about her name because she had outstanding warrants and had gone through the whole process using the false identity. I transported her to court for the recommencement of the trial. The senior constable's and the accused's smiles evaporated. In short order, the accused changed his plea to guilty and was sentenced to three years in the penitentiary. I felt vindicated, especially after the dressing down the judge had given to me.

As for the senior constable, I spoke to my patrol sergeant, who told me to write a memorandum expressing my concerns and give it to the inspector. I did, and never heard another thing about it. The constable became just one more person to be wary of.

Still in the same time period, I went to a domestic assault at an apartment in my district. A female alleged that she had been confined and assaulted by her common-law husband. She was marked up and bruised and provided a witness statement. She was very highly strung, however her story seemed accurate and credible. I located and arrested the suspect. I laid a number of charges, including unlawful confinement. In one of the rare cases where a detective was assigned follow-up on one of my files, a corporal was tasked with finishing the investigation. The next day, he confronted me, saying the case was shit and the complainant was a drugged out and vindictive bitch. The complaint left a phone message for me to call her shortly afterwards. I called her, and in her high-strung manner, she told me that the investigator had interrogated her, yelled at her, and basically called her a liar.

Apparently the investigator did not relay his convictions to the crown prosecutor, and a trial was set with a jury at the Court of Queen's Bench. The corporal had, however, relayed his concerns to the defence lawyer. When I took the stand, the defence lawyer came out swinging. I was questioned at length about the victim's drug use, information I did not have. This information the corporal had allegedly received and had not relayed to me. The lawyer was aggressive and asked a lot of questions I did not have the answers to. I left the stand red-faced and feeling like this was one of the lowest points in my police career.

Ultimately, the defence lawyer was able to convince the jury that the victim's allegations were figments of her drug-induced delusions, and his client was acquitted. My victim was shattered and said she would never report anything to the police again. The accused left the courtroom a free man. I got back to the station and was changing into my street uniform when I got a radio call asking if I'd been to the trial of my accused this morning. I radioed back that I had and that he'd been acquitted. The officer told me that the accused had hung himself right after leaving the court building.

I came up to get my patrol car and saw the corporal who had done the follow-up investigation, decided the man was not even worth telling, and went back to work.

Start of year twenty-six with the Saskatoon Police Service (courtesy Saskatoon Police Service)

12.

To Tell the Truth

The stereotype created by years of television shows and movies is that the police are supposed to hate lawyers, and rail against judges and unhelpful prosecutors. We are supposed to work in spite of them.

It is true, there are some lawyers I dislike, but I'm pretty sure I would dislike them in any job. There are some judges who let their politics influence their decisions. Some crown prosecutors are lazy. Then again, so are some police officers.

I've testified many times, and experience has taught me what a tough job these people have. My experiences with lawyers, judges, and prosecutors have been, for the most part, very good. We all work with people and try to apply the law in all its complexity in difficult situations.

My first trial was a summary offence trial when I was a military policeman. There are two types of trials in the military. The court-martial is for the more serious offences. Courts-martial are run by soldiers with legal training, much like civilian courts with a judge, a jury, and lawyers. Summary trials are trials before the commanding officer of a unit or base. Military personnel can choose in certain cases whether they wish to proceed by court-martial or by summary trial.

I was on patrol one night. It was very late, after 3 a.m., when I saw a vehicle at the petrol point. Basically, the petrol point was the filling point for all the military vehicles on the base. There were no exercises scheduled and no reason for anyone to be there, so I went to check it out. A corporal from the supply section was stealing gas and oil. I arrested him. While I was searching his vehicle, I located a loaded rifle under the seat.

The outcome could have been very different, and I learned a valuable lesson about officer safety. Nothing is as simple or as mundane as it appears. I took the corporal to the guardhouse and jailed him.

Trials happen quickly in the military if the accused chooses a summary trial. Within three days, I was notified to be at headquarters with my notes and to be prepared to testify. In the military police, you were required to escort your prisoner to the commanding officer's office. Escort is an understatement. You marched your prisoner at a defaulter's pace, 160 paces per minute, to the hallway outside of the commanding officer's door, then a crisp left, right, left until the prisoner is halted to await his fate.

I was so nervous my knees were knocking. It was my first trial, and I wanted everything to go right. I looked at my prisoner. He looked frightened. His career could be finished, and he had already invested eight years of his life with the Forces. A dishonourable discharge would have iced any of his future plans. The chief warrant officer of the base bellowed out, "Corporal, march the accused in."

I gulped and barked out the commands, "By the left quick march, left, right, left, right, halt." We were in the commanding officer's office.

Very formally, the commanding officer stated, "Corporal, give your evidence." I took out my notebook. I was shaking so much the pages flapped. The commanding officer looked at me and said, "Corporal, you are not on trial here." God bless him. I calmed down and testified. My thief was convicted and sent to prison. He was not kicked out because his record up to that time had been good. I hope he never made such a mistake again. The military was good that way. They invested a lot in their people and wanted due return.

A couple of years later, I was with the Saskatoon police and was called to testify at a trial on my days off. I cannot even remember what the trial was about now. I put on my only suit, and with my notebook and report in hand went to court. I showed up a few minutes ahead of everybody else. There was a judge still in the courtroom, wrapping up a previous proceeding. I went into the courtroom to familiarize myself with the layout. I nodded at the judge when I entered. He looked up and matter-of-factly asked me if I was represented by counsel. He must've thought I was the accused in the upcoming trial. I replied I was with the police.

I did not wear civilian clothes to court again for about fifteen years. By then I was satisfied that people knew who I was.

Credibility is everything when you're a police officer. There is no greater honour than to be known as a credible and honest officer. Every lesson is hard-learned, and experience is the best teacher in a courtroom.

Personally, I do not think police services take enough time to prepare officers for the rough-and-tumble world of the courts. Since ultimately the courts are the final test of your work, we should take the time to teach junior officers what we have learned.

What I've learned is that when you testify, tell the story truthfully and without having a personal stake in the outcome. Speak in simple terms; do not use police-specific language, and avoid codes and police jargon. If you don't know, you don't know—just say so. Do not offer your opinion unless the judge, and only the judge, asks you to. As a police officer, you have to remember that the judge has probably heard the same testimony hundreds of times from hundreds of police officers. Just tell your story. The truth has a certain ring to it in a courtroom. I don't know how to explain it. The truth sounds like the truth.

There was a horrific sexual assault trial that ended up in the Court of Queen's Bench. The husband had committed terrible acts against his wife. My partner and I had arrested him. The accused had a very prominent lawyer representing him. After I finished my testimony in chief, it was the turn of the defence lawyer to cross-examine me. He was very skillful and led me to where he thought he gained the biggest advantage. He wanted to prove the police were not diligent or thorough in their investigation. "The police," of course, was my partner and me. When the time was right, he asked why I did not seize the bedding from where the assault had taken place. I realized I had not as soon as he asked the question. I answered with the only answer I had, the truth. I answered that the act was so horrifying to me that at the time, I did not even think to seize the bedding. His client was convicted.

Another time, I was testifying at a weapons trial. The accused was charged with various firearms offences. As I testified, it became clear to me that I had laid the wrong charges. Not even thinking, I turned to the judge and told him so. He thanked me for my honesty and dismissed all the charges. The prosecutor was furious at me, but I did not mean to embarrass anyone. I had laid the wrong charge.

Sometimes I translate legal terms differently than their intended meanings. You'll often hear on television or a movie court drama a defence lawyer objecting to the admission of certain evidence because it is prejudicial to his client. From my experience, when a defence lawyer moves quickly to object to a certain piece of evidence or testimony because it's prejudicial to his client, the proper interpretation of the objection would be that the evidence or testimony is way too true.

Defence lawyers are on the dark side. A drug trial without a Charter of Rights argument is a guilty plea. A preliminary hearing is like fishing a day before the season opens. When a defence lawyer asks you a question requiring a long answer, they often object and say you are making a speech. What they really mean is, "Judge, make the officer stop talking because he's getting in too much evidence against my client."

Early in my career, a defence lawyer used a trick almost certainly reserved for inexperienced police officers. He brought the brother of an accused man in an assault trial to court dressed identically to the accused. When I was asked to identify the accused, of course I got the wrong brother. I was not mad. I was embarrassed. All I could think was, "Thanks for the lesson, counsellor. I will not make that mistake again."

There was a decision a few years ago called the *Gladue* decision. Basically, Canada's Supreme Court ruled that an Aboriginal accused's background should be considered in sentencing. The court was giving teeth to the *Criminal Code* section that provides that all reasonable alternatives to jail should be considered for offenders, with particular attention to the circumstances of Aboriginal offenders.

To me, nothing says you are a second-class citizen as a native person louder than saying we must give convicted criminals special consideration because they're native. I think the decision was condescending. While probably well intended, it serves the grievances of the basest people. If we as natives want to be treated as equal in all things, the law of the land is the most important one of all.

Judging the credibility of witnesses is a subjective exercise. Sometimes I wish we could introduce the offender's criminal record at the outset of the trial. There would be a lot fewer trials if we could. I am being facetious—I understand why we can't. Bad guys would not have a chance, and that's not fair. Being fair to criminals is the ground occupied by the unoffended—people who have never been the victim of crime.

You'll probably not hear this from many police officers, but I believe that for all its blemishes, our imperfect human creation is the fairest system you can have. When it works, it works well. In the end, who does a sentence serve? To be fair and reasonable should be the goal of anyone—police, judges, or lawyers—involved in the system.

13.

Murders and Major Crimes

I've been to more than twenty murders in my twenty-six years with the Saskatoon Police Service where I was the first or second officer at the scene. Murder is the ultimate criminal act. Its consequences can never be undone. Justice even when served never restores life, and the residual effects resonate across many lives. This is why the police response needs to be as close to perfect as possible. The complexity of the investigation, even of what seems to be a straight-forward crime, is daunting. I found the initial response to be one of the most challenging aspects of my career as a police officer.

My first murder was when I was still in recruit training with Saskatoon Police Service. My regular trainer had the day off. The staff sergeant told me I would ride with a senior officer. I called him on the radio and told him I had been assigned to work with him. He radioed back that he would be in to pick me up shortly. I was in the alley of the police station when I saw the officer pull in. As he stopped the car, a call came over the radio of an assault and injured person. The officer yelled at me to get in the car. I had barely clipped my seatbelt before the lights and sirens were going. At breakneck speeds, we went to the address. We braked hard and were out of the patrol car in seconds.

We went into a back yard, with uncut grass, overgrown bushes, and a fence in disrepair. There was a dilapidated couch with a woman passed out on it, and beside her sat a very large native man who appeared to be in his fifties and drunk. There was a smaller native man lying on the ground, and several other people pointing to the guy on the couch. Our finger-pointing witnesses also appeared to be drunk. There were several punctured cans of Lysol disinfectant lying in the area of the coach.

The whole thing seemed surreal. We quickly established that the guy on the couch had wanted the woman on the couch and that the male who was on the ground had tried to stop him. The man on the couch took exception to this and hit him in the back of the head with a two-metre-long and ten-centimetre-diameter fence post. His injuries were critical. Paramedics hustled to load the wounded man onto the stretcher. The senior officer ordered me to arrest the offender. I arrested and hand-cuffed him. He smelled strongly of Lysol mixed with water and was obviously drunk. I was then ordered to seize the fence post, which had a small spot of blood on it. The injured male was taken to the hospital. Our arrest and the fence post, which was on my lap, were transported to the station. Once both were secured, we went to the hospital to check on the injuries of our victim. We went into the trauma room where the medical team was trying to save the victim's life, but to no avail—he died shortly after we got there.

I shook my head. I had been to my first murder. I felt there was more to do. I felt there were more answers for us to find. Something... but apparently not. The suspect was charged with murder, pleaded guilty to manslaughter, and was sent to jail. There was no trial. No courtroom drama. I felt cheated.

One should always be careful what you wish for. I was too new to understand the tragedy that had occurred: two lives have been ruined by alcohol, both older, probably survivors of residential schools, lost in ad-dictions, and never part of mainstream society. I wish I had been mature enough to know the whole story.

In 1993, I was partnered with one of the quietest officers I've ever known. We had gone to police college together. It was a hot summer night, a payday, and it just felt like trouble. We only took four calls that night; they were all stabbings. The last one was one of the most tragic and scarring of my career. A call came in from a young girl, frantic and desperate. Her mother had been stabbed. We pulled up to the address, a basement apartment in a four-plex. The door was off the hinges, and a woman was lying on the kitchen floor with a huge wound to her chest. There was blood everywhere. I looked past her for threats or an offend-er and saw four children, all young, all screaming and crying in horror. Never before had I seen such horror and despair on the faces of children. I have seen many horrible things since, however this was one of the most challenging to my resolve. I looked at my partner and, as the paramedics came in, told him to go with the victim. He looked shaken to the core, but we still had a job to do.

I took the kids into a bedroom. The oldest was covered in blood. They were inconsolable. Shaking and barely able to control their limbs, they sat on the bed together while I tried to calm them down.

The paramedics and my partner hustled the mother to St Paul's Hospital, less than two blocks away. I overheard two constables on the radio say they saw a vehicle speeding away and ask whether they should go after it or come to the scene. I said to go after it, there's nothing to be done at the scene. We removed the children through a window so they would not have to see the carnage and blood that had been their mother. As I was waiting for another constable to come and take over the crime scene, I could not help notice how neat and well-kept the apartment was. There were plenty of books in the children's bedrooms, and everything there spoke of a mother's love for her children.

It turned out that the car the constables were after was the murderer's. They chased him until he blew the engine of his car some sixty kilometres later and they took him into custody. Those same constables had been called to this same address earlier in the night and had been waved away by the victim, who told them that she and her husband were just arguing and that she would be all right. I was relieved of the crime scene by another constable and came in to leave my report. The sun was up, and people were on their way to work. I went to the lunchroom, still shocked and too emotionally spent to make my notes. One of the clerical staff came in and asked me what I was still doing at work. I told her the story. She said nothing, started to cry, got up, and left.

The murderer made the children testify. I testified and broke down on the stand reliving the emotional initial response. The murderer sat in the court impassive and without remorse. I cannot remember ever wanting to throttle anyone more.

I started losing sleep, jumping at loud noises, and denying that all of this affected me. But my struggles were nothing compared to those children's struggles.

The murderer was convicted and sentenced to twenty-five years. He would have to serve eighteen years before being eligible for parole. The victim got life, and the children a lifetime of nightmares.

In the late fall of 1996, I was with a different partner. Our partnership lasted for six years; we had been working together for three years at the time. We were great partners. We knew intuitively when to act. We could read each other's cues and together made hundreds of arrests.

It was night shift. The sun had set early; it was cold and moonless when a call came in of an assault in progress in the 300 block of Avenue H South. We rolled up and pulled into the lane where the caller had said the assault was happening. As I turned the patrol car, the headlights flashed over several people, and a man lying on the ground.

People started running, but not before dropping a twenty-kilogram bag of dried cement on the head of the man on the ground. My partner yelled at me not to run over the victim as I braked to a halt and jumped out to chase the closest suspect. As I ran by the victim, I could see his skull was crushed, and the heat from his body was steaming into the cold night air. My suspect ran into a yard. I knew the resident there was hoarder. His yard was full of wire and scrap metal. Not being able to use my flashlight for fear of exposing myself to an ambush slowed me down. I could hear the radio going off constantly as other units responded. I couldn't get on the air to give my suspect's direction of travel. I entered the backyard with my pistol at the ready and began to search.

I heard a vehicle screech to a halt and more yelling. I got to the street, and it was empty except for police and civilians. A police K-9 unit arrived, and we began to track for a while, until the entire neighbourhood came out of their homes to see what the commotion was about and ruined our track. I went back to my partner's location. He was with the paramedics and the very obviously dead victim. It turned out that I had arrested him several times before. The amount of damage to his face and skull made him unrecognizable. The paramedics were visibly upset.

The K-9 officer and I began to look around and found a blood trail which led back to an address on 20th Street, thirty or forty metres from where the body lay. There was blood on the back door and on the step. We decided there could be more injured persons in the residence and we were duty-bound to check. I swung the door open and announced, "Police." Inside, there were two women and a man with blood on their clothing. We detained them and sent them in for questioning.

As it turned out, the detectives seized the clothes and questioned and released the suspects, all of whom had criminal warrants and should have stayed in custody anyway. Of course, it was our last night shift when the murder occurred, and we were left to our thoughts for four days.

When I returned to work, the homicide detectives were confrontational and accusatory. They soundly criticized the Patrol response. In my opinion, they had made mistakes the night of the murder and were trying to deflect them back onto the responding patrol members, namely me and my partner. This was not the first time I had encountered this. I went on the attack and told them what I had seen and heard. The first thing homicide detectives do when they arrive at a murder is to interview the first officers at the scene. I was never interviewed. They could not even put their personal feelings about me aside to do their job. I said my piece and never heard anything more about it. I felt like I was still in an uphill battle and there was no one at the top who wanted me there.

Eventually, the matter came to trial. I was confident that I had done my job. How confident the detectives were showed in the plea bargain. All three accused pleaded guilty to manslaughter. The longest sentence was five years. The victim and the victim's family were, in my opinion, served a very thin slice of justice. It was a horrific crime, the kind of scene it is almost impossible to totally lock out of your mind. I was satisfied I did my job, however, and the outcome was ultimately out of my hands.

I went to a call of a male stabbed in an alley in the Pleasant Hill neighbourhood of Saskatoon. I was by myself, and I arrived to find a man lying outside of a doorway in a lane. He was screaming in pain. I could not see a visible wound. I asked him to calm down and show me where he had been stabbed. He opened his shirt and showed me a small wound in his chest. I told him to calm down—I had seen people stabbed far worse who did not yell as much. What I didn't realize was that the knife had penetrated his heart and he was fighting for his life. When the paramedics and firefighters arrived, they realized how serious the injury was, and they quickly loaded him in the ambulance. Within a moment, we were on our way to St Paul's Hospital, only a few blocks east of where he had been stabbed.

Once at the hospital, the emergency room doctor did his best to stop the bleeding enough so the patient could be transferred to the Royal University Hospital. As soon as they could, they loaded the victim back into an ambulance and, with a firefighter's finger in the hole in the victim's heart to staunch the bleeding, off we went. As soon as we arrived at the hospital, we went straight into the trauma room. A team of doctors used chest splitters to open the victim's chest and used small electric paddles to keep his heart going.

The battle went on for hours. I was relieved and returned to the station to leave my report.

The victim clung to life and lingered, never regaining consciousness, before dying the next day. A suspect was later arrested and charged with the murder.

The suspect's lawyer argued at trial that the delay caused by taking the victim to the first available hospital rather than the University Hospital, which was better equipped to deal with the trauma, was the cause of his death. When he cross-examined me, I felt he was easily the most arrogant and ignorant lawyer I had dealt with. He created enough doubt that the jury acquitted the suspect. The man who was acquitted was a gang member and a couple of years later committed a murder in Prince Albert. The victim had nothing to do with gangs and was simply in the wrong place at the wrong time.

I have always regretted my words to the victim. I learned as much as I could about penetrating wounds afterwards. His murder steered me away from the creeping emotional detachment I was starting to feel toward male victims of crime.

In September of 2001, on a night shift, my partner and I were taking a missing persons report when a call came in of a shooting in a bar a few blocks away. We ran back to our car and arrived within seconds. As we arrived, I could see a man with his arm outstretched, holding what appeared to be a gun, shooting at a group of people. The people were ducking and moving away. The suspects were two brothers and another man. They began to run as soon as we braked to a stop. My partner went after one brother and I went after the other.

The bar was attached to a pawn shop with a fenced compound. My suspect ran from the front of the bar and was rounding the corner of the compound. I was about five metres behind him when the pawn shop owner, who was in the compound, yelled at me that the guy I was chasing was the shooter and had a gun.

I rounded the corner and yelled at suspect to stop. He turned around. I could see the holster stuffed in the front of his pants. I had my pistol aimed directly at his chest. I ordered him to show me his hands and to get on the ground. He stood there defiantly and said, "Fuck you, Ernie, go hard." I started to pull the trigger. When I was about two pounds of trigger pressure away from firing, the suspect threw himself to the ground. Very carefully, I released the trigger, and the suspect lived to go to jail.

The victim had been shot in the stomach inside the bar. He was not the intended target but was shot when he tried to grab the gun. As backup units arrived and took custody of my arrest, I could see a revolver in the grass along the fence line of the compound five metres from where my suspect went to the ground. It was loaded, and two rounds had been fired from it. Before we could secure the crime scene, the bar staff mopped the floor and tried to resume business. The clientele at the bar were not all law-abiding citizens, so other officers had the difficult task of trying to get statements from them. Investigators from Major Crimes and the Forensics Identification section were called in. The victim had been taken to hospital and would live.

About a month later, I got a phone message asking me to call the victim. I called him back and he thanked me. Apparently, he was a difficult witness for the detectives because it went against the street code to co-operate with the police. My shooter came to trial a couple months later at Court of Queen's Bench. As I was testifying, I described how he held the gun canted to the side and called it gangster style. The prosecutor had me go through how close the suspect was to being shot. The accused testified in his own defence. He self-proclaimed himself as a gang member and then used the time-honoured defence of "It wasn't me." He was convicted and sentenced to five years. The victim recovered.

In July 2010, we were having a busy hot summer night. I had been the patrol sergeant in central district for a couple years at the time. The call came in of a drunk driver who had struck and dragged a woman with a pick-up truck outside of a nightclub, injuring her. The suspect was identified by name, and we were all on the lookout for him and his vehicle. Moments later, the call came in that a male had been shot in a home in the west end of Saskatoon. I went up to that location to give the other sergeant a hand. There was an ambulance outside of the home. The victim had been shot three times.

On the way there, I learned it was the same man who been shot nine years before. He was in the back of the ambulance, yelling, swearing, and being unco-operative with the paramedics. He was obviously in a lot of pain. I got in the back with him and told him to settle down, he had been shot before. He called me by name and said he would.

I rode to the hospital with him. Once medical staff told me he was not going to die, I left him in their care. While I was with him, the other officers had identified the shooter as the driver of the truck who had dragged the woman. The suspect was at a local motorcycle gang clubhouse. We didn't know if he still had the gun with him or not.

The night was ending and the first grey fingers of dawn were approaching when we set up a loose surveillance on his vehicle. One of the constables found some high ground that gave him a concealed position to observe the front of the clubhouse. The sun was almost completely up when the suspect came strolling back to his vehicle. We took him down hard before he got to his truck. He did not have the gun on his person. Once he was handcuffed and in my car, officers wanted to search the vehicle. I told them no and that we would get a search warrant. Major Crime investigators later found the gun covered in blood in the truck.

The suspect pleaded guilty to attempted murder and received a five-year sentence. The victim, who now had the dubious distinction of being shot twice while I was working, recovered.

In July 2005, I was with the Street Crime unit. I came to work and learned that a man had been murdered in his basement apartment in the Riversdale area. I knew the victim and had been at his address many times over the years. It was a multi-dwelling house. The owner always seemed to rent the suites to heavy drinkers. I went down to the Major Crimes section and asked the investigators if they minded if I went to the crime scene and poked around. There were almost all new members in the section, and they had a totally different way of doing business. They told me the crime scene had been released, and I was free to go there if I wanted to. I went back to the office to see if anybody was interested in coming with me. Nobody was, and I got the distinct impression that the murder of a drunk did not interest them.

I went to the alley behind the address where I had been many times as a patrol officer. The door to the victim's apartment was standing open. I approached slowly and could hear someone inside the dead man's apartment. I entered and saw another male, a heavy drinker who lived in the apartment on the top floor the building. He was helping himself to the stereo and dishes. I told him to put them back. He told me that the victim was dead and would no longer need them. He had been drinking. I warned him one last time to put the stuff back, and he refused.

At this point, I arrested him for break and enter and theft. To my surprise, he began to fight me hard. I had not cleared the apartment and didn't know if he was with anybody else, so I used OC spray (*Oleoresin capsicum*, or pepper spray) on him, pushed him to the ground, and handcuffed him. I had never seen that level of aggression from him before. After I had advised him of his rights, I transported him to detention.

Once he was booked in, I took him to an interview room. I was going to ask him why he had resisted arrest and why he seemed so stressed. Then it dawned on me: I asked him if he had been interviewed by any of the patrol officers or investigators about the murder.

He bowed his head and said no. I then asked him what he knew about the murder of his friend. He told me that from his third-floor apartment, he had seen a male coming out of his friend's window. He didn't know the name of the male, but he knew the name of the suspect's mother. I left him in the interview room and called the lead investigator on the homicide and told him I had an eyewitness. The detectives came upstairs and took my arrest. I went back to the Street Crime unit office and left my report.

In December 2005, a man was stabbed to death in the Meadow Green neighbourhood of Saskatoon. The suspects were identified as persons of interest shortly afterwards. Two other members the Street Crime unit and I located them walking on the street. They were taken into custody and later charged with the murder. One of the males was the suspect from the murder in the Riversdale apartment. Ultimately, the suspect was charged with both killings. For the second killing, the two other men were also charged. The suspect was acquitted of the Meadow Green murder at trial but pleaded guilty to the Riversdale murder. He received an eight-year sentence for manslaughter. He went on to be involved in a third killing at the Saskatchewan Penitentiary in Prince Albert.

The lesson I learned here was that you're never too important to interview someone, even a habitual drunk, and if you think you are, it is your loss. I think the lesson wasn't lost on the other members of the unit, some of whom have gone on to become some of the best investigators with the Saskatoon Police Service.

In April 2006, I was appointed acting sergeant in the central district with a new platoon. We were having a busy summer night in June 2006—everybody was tied up at calls, and the calls just kept coming. It was almost 6 a.m. when I cleared an assault call. I could see all of my guys were tied up, and I checked the pending calls queue on the computer. I saw a call of an injured person in the Mayfair Heights area of Saskatoon. The call said a male had been stabbed in the chest. Experience by this time had taught me that stab wounds to the chest are almost always serious. I had learned over the years that the chances of surviving a penetrating wound to the heart are less than 10 per cent, even in an operating room. I made it to the call in a minute even though it was a couple miles from the call I had just cleared.

When I got there, I could see two ambulances and a row of people proned out face down on the ground. There were three paramedics standing over them. I can honestly say I had never seen anything like it before. The lead paramedic quickly told me that they had responded to the injured male call and had taken a man from inside the house to their unit, where he died. As I was talking to him, a woman on the ground told me that she had killed her common-law husband, and that the other people had nothing to do with it. I quickly called in that we had a murder and arrested the woman.

Within moments, several cars from my shift and the oncoming day shift were at the scene. I turned over the arrested woman to some constables. The other people on the ground were stood up and identified. There were several children with them as well. The mosquitoes were coming hard, but I couldn't let the people go back into the house as it was a crime scene. I got a city bus to come to our location. Once the people were on the bus, I asked two constables to clear the house to ensure no one else was in it. They radioed that they had found what appeared to be the murder weapon. By then, I was so tired I could hardly spit. Eventually, the day shift sergeant arrived at the scene and took over. I went into the Major Crimes office and briefed them on everything that had transpired. I left my report and went home.

Within twenty-four hours, the woman had been charged with second-degree murder. As tragic as this murder was, it was my first big test as sergeant. It could not have gone much better. The suspect was arrested. The murder weapon was recovered, and no one else got hurt. The common-law wife eventually pleaded guilty to manslaughter and received a sentence of four years. The paramedics are still out there working, and I don't know if they ever had an experience like this one again.

In November 2007, I responded to a call of a male with head injuries in the Riversdale neighbourhood of Saskatoon. Two constables and I arrived at almost the same time. One of the constables was still in training. The male who had called the police told us he had been in a fight with the injured male. I immediately asked two constables to detain the male and record everything he said. I went into the house and saw a male lying on the floor by the back door in the kitchen area. It was obvious that there had been a struggle as furniture was overturned and there was broken glass everywhere. As I got up to the male, I could see that his head appeared to be crushed. I didn't think he was alive. I told the responding units to stay outside. When the paramedics came to the door, I instructed them to come directly to me and to make as little disturbance as possible. To my surprise, the first paramedic who checked the victim indicated he had a pulse, and they quickly put him on a stretcher and evacuated him.

He later died in hospital. The murder weapon was a heavy mug. The suspect and the victim had a long and violent history. The young constable-in-training made sixty pages of notes before the suspect was turned over to investigators. The suspect was convicted at a trial at the Court of Queen's Bench in Saskatoon and received a twelve-year sentence.

In April 2008, there was a murder in the Pleasant Hill neighbourhood of Saskatoon. The murder happened on my days off, but it happened at the notorious four-plex I'd been to several hundred times in my career. I went to the lead investigator and asked him if he minded if I made some inquiries. This is how much things had changed since 1987: he told me to go ahead.

I knew the people in the apartment facing the alley, and I went to see them first. The couple told me that one of the residents of the apartment where the killing had taken place had been taken to hospital by ambulance a couple of hours prior to me coming to see them. When I asked what had happened, they told me that one of the two occupants of the apartment where the murder had occurred had assaulted the other.

I told them I would get back to them and went out to my patrol car and called Communications. They confirmed that there had been an ambulance call to that address a couple of hours earlier. The paramedics had cancelled the police and transported a male to a hospital. I went to the hospital and located the victim. He told me that the other occupant of the apartment had stomped on his leg and was trying to blame him for the murder the night before.

I called the lead investigator and told him what was going on. He told me to keep on going. After I got enough information from the male at the hospital, I went back to the address and arrested his roommate for common assault. I transported him into the Saskatoon Police Service detention unit, and after he was booked in, I went back to the hospital and brought the alleged assault victim from earlier in the day in for a statement. I had known both of these men for years and had arrested them both several times before. Once the alleged victim was in an interview room, the lead investigator gave me a tape recorder and told me to arrest him for the murder that had occurred the night before. By this time, I was into overtime, and I recruited my former partner, who was still on my old platoon, to assist me. I arrested the alleged assault victim for murder, advised him of his rights, and put him on a phone to a lawyer.

The lead investigator then told me to arrest his roommate for murder. My former partner and I effected the arrest and hooked him up with lawyer. It was the first time I ever arrested two people for murder in the same day. It turned out that both of these men had been drinking with a male from northern Saskatchewan in their apartment. They took exception to something he said and beat him to death. It was senseless. One of the accused was a small man, and he seemed to revel in the fact that he was able to kill someone. Both men pleaded guilty to manslaughter and received seven-year sentences. The lesson once again was to talk to everyone regardless of their station in life.

October 2009—Halloween—a call about an injured person came in toward the end of our day shift. He was injured in a fight outside of a downtown liquor store. As it was Halloween, there was a steady stream of customers getting ready for the night's festivities. The initial call indicated that the injured person had attempted to assault an elderly man. I rolled up, and there was an ambulance in front of the store. There was a male in the back on a stretcher fighting with the paramedics who were trying to treat him. I went into the ambulance and restrained him. At this point, I thought he was the instigator. Another constable came to the scene and rode to the hospital with the male in the ambulance. I went into the liquor store to try to sort out what had happened and to see if there were any witnesses. While I was asking questions, the constable who had gone to the hospital radioed me and told me that the victim from liquor store was coding. At first I thought it was the elderly gentleman who had apparently been attacked by the guy in the ambulance. It turned out that it was the guy in the ambulance, and he died.

This now became a murder investigation. The victim and several other people had arrived outside the liquor store in a van. The driver of the van, who only looked elderly, and the victim became involved in an argument, which led to a fight. The driver kicked and punched the victim, causing internal damage that led to his death. The suspect had gone into the liquor store after the assault and made a purchase. I had the liquor store employees save the surveillance footage of him coming in but forgot to ask how he paid. Luckily, other constables on my shift identified the suspect from the surveillance video and he was quickly arrested. Subsequently, he pleaded guilty to manslaughter and received a three-year sentence. I learned you're never too old to learn.

A lot of blood and a world of pain come with murders. Murders will always be part of the fabric of any society—there is no way to prevent crimes of passion. How well we react and investigate them is how we will be judged as police officers at the end of the day.

Almost all the victims of murders I have seen have been natives, once again a direct consequence of the area I worked in. In the early part of my career, I saw victims and families treated poorly; in my view, indifferent investigators and Crown and defence lawyers made plea bargains for expediency. I would shake my head and wonder when we would learn.

I would like to say that it was no one's fault—things were the way they were, and it couldn't be helped. I'd like to but I can't.

Slowly, though, I could see the changes over twenty-six years. Inquiries helped, but other police officers saw the same things I did and worked within the system to change things. I was too deeply mired in the front lines to see the gradual and positive changes taking place. After all the frustration and helplessness I felt, I am confident now that the full resources of the police and Crown are utilized to bring closure and justice to the victims of homicide regardless of race or social standing.

You don't get to choose where your crime scene will be. (Courtesy Saskatoon Police Service)

14.

Dangerous Pursuits

Movies and television have turned police chases into entertainment. The truth is that they are dangerous, and only in the most extreme circumstances should they be allowed to happen. When I first started with the Saskatoon Police Service, pursuits were fairly common. I'd be lying if I said they were not exciting and challenging. Once again, experience is the cruelest of teachers.

In 1996, several bodies were found in the area of a golf course outside of Saskatoon. It was publicly announced that a serial killer was at work. Because the bodies were found out of town, the RCMP was running the investigation. Patrol officers with the Saskatoon Police Service were not given any information as to a possible suspect, so we knew nothing—anybody or any vehicle we stopped could be the serial killer.

It was around 1 a.m. and I was paired up with a young fellow who had about the same amount of service as I did. We were talking about our newborns—his son and my second daughter, born three weeks earlier—when I saw a four-wheel-drive pickup truck blow through a stop sign.

I got behind it and hit the overhead lights, signaling it to stop. The driver floored the powerful truck, and the chase was on. Through yards and alleys and residential streets, reaching speeds of one hundred kilometres an hour, this guy was determined not to stop. I told my white-knuckled partner that this could be our serial killer. When the driver realized that he was not going to lose us on the residential streets, he hit the highway and headed out of Saskatoon at speeds of up to two hundred kilometres an hour.

This would never happen now. Spike or stop sticks would have been employed, or the Saskatoon Police Service aircraft would have taken over. Back then, we didn't have any those things. So this dangerous and crazy pursuit carried on, out onto the highway and into the blackness of the night. We were receiving frantic radio calls to watch out for deer. The deer would have been vapourized on impact, but probably we would have killed ourselves as well at the speeds we were going. After twenty-six minutes of total mental and physical commitment, we reached a provincial park. The suspect blew past the gate, realized it was a campground, and did a U-turn. We passed each other at one hundred kilometres an hour. I braked, pulled a U-turn, and kept after him. Thank God for the engineers and designers who made these vehicles to be able to withstand such abuse. I'm sure they never imagined the vehicles were ever going to be abused in such a manner.

At the twenty-seventh minute of this madness, the suspect rammed a RCMP vehicle that had become involved. The RCMP vehicle spun out and went into the ditch. It came through the ditch at the same time the suspect hit the patrol wagon (which had a terrible centre of balance and should never been there in the first place) and caused it to flip onto its roof. The RCMP constable's vehicle came out of the ditch and crashed into my door. I swore—twenty-eight minutes, and I had made it through with no damage to my vehicle up until then.

The suspect's vehicle had been disabled with all the smashing and crashing. I could see officers moving in to take him into custody. My door was smashed and jammed, and I had to crawl out over the computer and out the passenger door.

The RCMP officer appeared to be okay. I went to the patrol wagon, which was on its roof and was leaking gas onto the road. The constables were still in their seatbelts, hanging upside down. I watched as the gas started to pool and then saw a sergeant with a lit cigarette in his mouth strolling toward us. Three or four of us yelled for him to back off. I reached in and cut the seatbelt of one of the officers, who promptly landed on his head—with all the adrenaline, I had forgotten to warn him.

The suspect, by now in handcuffs, was turned over to me. Because I was in the pursuit car, he was my prisoner. I arrested him for dangerous driving and, smelling alcohol, made a breath demand on him. He was drunk and defiant. Muscular and used to getting his way, he was a very difficult arrest. He resisted arrest, and soon had the marks on him to prove it.

We had to take him to the hospital before he could provide samples of his breath. When we arrived at St Paul's Hospital, my suspect continued to be aggressive and unco-operative, not just with the police but with the medical staff as well. It turned out he was not the serial killer but a serial impaired driver. He worked on oil rigs and had money to burn and pretty much did not care about the here and now. Everyone was all right, just bumps and bruises and wrecked cars. It was the stuff movies are made of.

The suspect was convicted of impaired driving and failing to stop for the police, and received a twenty-two-month jail sentence. The defence tried to raise the accusation that the suspect had been roughed up upon his arrest and had to be taken to the hospital for treatment. I testified about how he spit at a doctor in the emergency room. He did not get a lot of sympathy.

February 14, 1999, was a Sunday night shift. Sunday nights were usually quiet—good nights to catch up on your files and recharge your batteries. I was at work and feeling sorry for myself because it was Valentine's Day and my wife was home alone with the kids again. The dispatcher read out the description of a stolen car we were to be on the lookout for. I was working with a female constable who had about the same amount of time on the job as I did at that point, twelve years. We were in the Riversdale area of Saskatoon when two officers called in on the radio and said they were in pursuit of the stolen car that had been read out moments earlier. I was driving and pointed our patrol car in the direction of the pursuit, hoping to assist. Officers in pursuit radioed that the vehicle was approaching 19th Street, going southbound on Second Avenue.

We came to the intersection of 19th Street and Second Avenue and saw the stolen car ram the pursuing patrol car. It then hit the patrol sergeant's vehicle, which was trying to box in suspect's vehicle. The stolen car broke free of the collisions and started northbound on Second Avenue. We were now the primary pursuit vehicle. The vehicle, an older midsized North American car, quickly gained speed. The back door opened. I thought at first that the backseat passenger was going to shoot at us, but then I realized he was trying to jump out. The driver of the stolen car accelerated. We followed for one city block. I told my partner that it was too dangerous. She agreed. I started to let off the gas.

The stolen car carried on northbound and everything seemed to go into slow motion. I saw a red car going from east to west on 22nd Street. The stolen vehicle was approaching a solid red light at a high rate of speed. The red car started through the intersection on a green light, unaware of the impending collision.

The stolen car and its occupants hit the red car on the driver's side. I could hear the impact over the blaring radio and sirens. Debris and smoke filled the air. We rolled up and jumped out of our patrol car. There were several patrol cars in the area, all of them occupied by members of my platoon of the last twelve years.

The radio was going crazy, and there were frantic calls for ambulances. I went to the stolen car with my gun drawn. I did not want any of these people escaping. The front seat passenger was unconscious. The driver was winded and appeared to be injured. A rear seat passenger had gone headfirst through the windshield. The second backseat passenger had a lap belt on and his back appeared to be broken. Someone came up to me and guided my pistol back into the holster, telling me it was all right and no one was going anywhere.

Ambulances and fire trucks began arriving. My mind was reeling. I knew we had to establish some semblance of control and start organizing things. I remember telling the paramedics not to touch the suspects until the innocent victims were transported. You could tell from everyone's faces the enormity of what had just happened. As we tried to absorb the violence and tragedy of what we had just witnessed, we still had to do our jobs. The patrol sergeant rolled up, and I remember telling him what we needed and what needed to be covered. The normal procedure was to have an officer ride in the ambulance with the driver of a vehicle involved in a criminal offence, but there were six injured persons. They were being loaded into ambulances. Between the paramedics, firefighters, and victims, there was no room for a police officer to ride with the suspects.

I went to the hospital. Officers who had been with the victims from the red car were there. By this time, information had started to come in. The people in the red car were a high school principal and his wife from a small town close to Saskatoon. They were in Saskatoon celebrating Valentine's Day. The husband died at the scene, and his wife died in hospital. The suspects in the stolen car had suffered serious injuries, except the driver, but they would all live.

There was lots of hugging and crying as we started trying to cope with what happened.

I knew we still had to do our job. I don't know where the resolve came from, but I found it and went to gather information on the suspects. The driver of the stolen car was a big guy, thick in the chest and about one hundred kilograms—two hundred plus pounds. He was whiney and knew he had made a huge mistake and was trying to downplay his responsibility, blaming the front-seat passenger for stealing the car. I was in the room while they were treating the driver and it looked like he coded. I watched him dispassionately while they worked on him and revived him. There was not a lot more for me to do at the hospital. I had been telling everyone that I would leave the report, and everyone needed to focus on the job at hand in spite of what had occurred.

I went back to the station and was having a cigarette at the side door when the chief and some executive officers showed up. I was impressed, and even more impressed when the chief asked if I was all right. I lied and said I was. Maybe not a lie, but certainly not totally true—I was not all right. I asked him not to let the media make us into the bad guys on this one. He did not. He came out later the next day aggressive and articulate, railing against the driver who was out on bail for robbery and other violent offences. He criticized the courts and even the registered owner for leaving her keys in the vehicle while it was parked and running—a little harsh, but that simple action allowed the suspects to steal her vehicle and started a chain of events that killed two innocent people.

The rest of the night was spent doing reports and gathering evidence and doing all the things we needed to do.

We met on our days off at a McDonald's restaurant where there was a play structure—almost all of us had small kids. We did not talk too much about what had happened. We just needed to be together. The crash had happened on our last night shift. I told everyone not to listen to the media or local talk shows. I tried not to listen to anything. My sister, a police officer in Ontario, called me and told me not to talk to anyone and to get a lawyer. I told her we did not have a civilian oversight organization like Ontario did, and that we were not so aggressive in the West trying to charge police every time a serious incident happened.

The first shift back was a day shift. The staff sergeant acted as if nothing happened. In fact, I did not remember him having any role at all the night of the pursuit or any time afterward. He even assigned us all to be with different partners, and we went back to work.

I had struggled with the shock of dealing with other things before, but this incident was by far the worst. I did not acknowledge it at first, but over time I came to recognize it for what was. My wife and family struggled to cope with the new husband and father who could not sleep properly, who was quick to get angry and drank too much.

Eventually you level out, but in the end you are changed—a different man, until the next trauma. And there will always be more trauma if you stay in Patrol.

The families of the victims were the most gracious and understanding people I've ever seen. Some of the officers from our shift night went to the funerals. They were all stronger than I was in that regard. All I heard from them was how dignified the family was. Their strength of character helped us all.

The trial or preliminary hearing came several months later. I was testifying and became anxious and shook. I started crying while reliving the whole thing, and it took me several moments to regain my composure enough to finish my testimony. The judge asked if I needed more time. I said no and pushed on.

The driver was sentenced to seven years. I understand our judiciary is bound by case law and precedents set in similar cases. The sentencing range is predetermined. But at what point does this much carnage and pain become a measurable outcome, and who has received justice at the end of the day?

15.

Training Ground

In the centre of the Riversdale neighbourhood, there was a (now closed) Chinese restaurant with two floors of apartments over it. I don't know when it was built, but probably in the 1930s or 1940s. The owner had an apartment suite in the back of the restaurant on the main floor. He had been there as long as I'd been a police officer in Saskatoon. The upstairs apartments were one- and two-bedroom suites. There was a common bathroom on each floor. The main entrance to the apartments was on 20th Street. You entered and had to climb a set of steep stairs to access the apartments. At the end of each hallway, there was an old-fashioned metal fire escape with a drop-down ladder. When I first started with the Saskatoon police, I had no idea how many times I would be in this building over the next twenty-six years.

I was walking the beat the first time I went into the restaurant. It was like I had found a gold mine.

I was used to drug trafficking and crimes at the hotels, but there were times when I could not find some of the criminals I was looking for. I knew they were still active but had no idea where they were hanging their hats.

They were at this restaurant, conducting their usual business. The restaurant was ideal for street-level trafficking. It was poorly lit, and the seating was in booths. There was only one entrance, and there was a partition in front of the bathroom doors.

The restaurant became a regular stop for me, and I would arrest people on warrants or drug charges nearly every night. The owner expressed frustration with criminals but basically threw his hands up, saying there was nothing he could do.

Eventually, he closed the restaurant. I started going to calls in the apartment upstairs. I'll never forget the first time I went in the front door and up the stairs. The smell of urine, unwashed bodies, and desperation was overpowering. Because the apartments shared common bathrooms on each floor, the rent was low, and Social Services rented every apartment.

For some of the most desperate alcoholics, this was the only accommodation they could find. For the most part, there was a sense of community amongst the drunks in the building. It was nothing to find six or seven people living together in a one-bedroom apartment. They shared all manner of concoctions: Lysol, hairspray, mouthwash, and store-bought alcohol when they could afford it—all substances to numb them to their unfortunate circumstances. The trouble came when they ran out of alcohol or when they allowed outsiders into their circle of inebriation.

For the most part, the occupants of the apartment building were middle-aged, long-term alcoholics who lived on social assistance and augmented their income by binning. Binning was going out early in the morning to pick recyclable cans and bottles. Most of them had their own specific territory, and others usually respected it.

Most of the residents there were emaciated and in poor physical condition because of their alcoholism, so when a younger or stronger person was allowed to join them, the residents were quickly victimized. They were easy targets, especially around welfare days.

Every city has a building like this, a building that tests the levels of tolerance and compassion of the community. Often it comes down to out of sight, out of mind. I kind of adopted the place and the unfortunate souls who occupied it.

I would police them hard. If they had warrants, I would arrest them right away. If they committed offences, I would charge them without a second thought. But I also cared about their welfare and made frequent checks of the building. I went there so frequently that the owner gave me a key to the front door and a list of the tenants.

Like the tenants, the building continued to deteriorate, and every time I went in, the surroundings had become bleaker and bleaker. There were holes in the walls, and people frequently urinated in the hallways. They would throw garbage out their windows so it landed on the roofs of neighbouring buildings. In the summer, the place would reek. There was no air-conditioning, and people left the windows open, which brought flies and other insects into the already volatile and filthy environment.

Over the years, I built up enough of a rapport with the residents so that even though they constantly told me they hated me, they reported crimes.

It seemed every year a bully or pair of bullies would come on the scene. They would beat people up and rob the tenants. One particular man was especially evil. He had a tattoo of a cross in the middle of his forehead. He was strongly built and all predator. He beat and robbed his way through the building. Everyone was afraid him. He raped one woman, who bravely gave me a statement. When my partner and I arrested him, I told him that I knew what he was and that eventually he would end up doing twenty-five years for murder. He said he would do twenty-five years for killing me. My partner charged him with uttering threats to cause death.

The victim of the sexual assault died before he came to trial. The crown prosecutor bravely tried to run the trial with the written statement of the victim. It wasn't enough, and he was discharged for want of a live witness. He moved out of Saskatoon shortly afterwards. His story, I am sure, is not over yet.

I took pride in the fact that I knew everyone and that I could go into that wretched place as often as I did. I also felt sad when one of those people passed. One summer while trying to escape the heat, some of the guys were drinking on the fire escape. One of the men went to climb down the ladder to go to the next floor for more drinking, but he slipped and fell headfirst onto the sidewalk below. He was over 100 kilograms— easily 240 pounds—and he fell right in front of another patrolman. He died from his injuries. Still the place kept running itself. I would take calls of sudden deaths when one of the renters or their friends succumbed to the abuses they had put their bodies through. One year, I even took a call on Christmas Day. The man died on a filthy mattress, in a room with no furniture, by himself on Christmas Day, surrounded by garbage and empty bottles of mouthwash.

There was one apartment in the building that was different from all the rest. It was occupied by a grandmother who kept her apartment immaculately clean and even had family who would visit her there. It was the only apartment where you could smell something other than vile. She stayed there for years, until a street gang known as the Native Syndicate, or NS, began to move in.

There had always been a level of violence and criminality in the building. There was even a murder. But it was almost always alcohol-related. It was a difficult place to police, and sometimes it was a physically repulsive working environment. With the coming of the gang, it sank to a new level of depravity. From difficult it went straight to dangerous, and as a newly promoted sergeant, it became my training ground. I would bring my officers with me frequently to test their mettle and empathy in trying circumstances. And tested it would be.

However meager their apartment, it was their home. Gang members would take over an apartment and force the occupants to leave, usually to the apartment across the hall. They would then begin to deal drugs out of the commandeered apartment. Drugs brought in a new level of violence and increased its frequency.

Twice in one year when entering the apartment building, the constables and I walked into people brandishing weapons. One had a club and a loaded syringe in his hand and tried to run when he saw us. He was tackled in the hallway outside the door of the grandmother who kept her apartment so immaculate. The second time, I think the suspect was going to collect a drug debt from somebody in the apartment because he was walking around with brass knuckles on. He was taken down in the hallway and arrested. Once we went to an apartment to arrest a gang member on an outstanding warrant. The gang member jumped out the third-floor window and landed on the roof of an adjacent restaurant. He then went in an open window on the second floor and escaped. An informant told me that gang members were planning and practising their escapes because of the frequency of my platoon's visits.

The building itself continued to deteriorate. Gang members had scrawled graffiti over everything, especially in the stairwells and hallways. There were literally hundreds of used and dirty syringes throughout the building. They were everywhere: in the bathrooms, in the hallways, and even in the false ceilings. The place had been a biohazard for years and had only gotten more dangerous. Still, it was a perfect place to acclimatize young constables to poverty and depravity. Some would only go there if they had to; others on my shift came to see it as the same challenge that I did.

There were other places requiring frequent police attendance, but this one gave me the opportunity every time I went into it to see how quickly my officers were able to think on their feet. It also gave me the opportunity to see how they dealt with the poorest people. I almost always walked away pleased at what I saw. There should be no prissy in patrol work.

Finally, after years and years of arrests and visits, the owner evicted everyone and shut the place down. There were several visits by the fire department and citations for health and safety violations, which helped to move the process along. The place is up for sale now.

Testifying at the Stonechild Inquiry (courtesy The StarPhoenix)

16.

Young Man Frozen

In late November 1990, I never missed an issue of the local paper. In my early years with the Saskatoon Police Service, I had a hunger for the news and cared how the media portrayed us. It was my last day off, and I picked up the paper from a confectionery in the lobby of our apartment building. I read through the headlines, none of which I can remember now, and came across a small article describing what sounded like a death by misadventure. A young man had been found frozen to death by two workers in a field in the north end of Saskatoon's industrial area. I perked up and was immediately intrigued by the lack of detail. I decided I would find out what the real story was when I returned to work.

When I got to work, no one seemed to know a lot about the young man's death. Eventually, I found somebody in the station who knew that the dead person had been identified as Neil Stonechild. I recognized the name, but not having had a lot of dealings with him, I was not seized by the tragedy. I knew his younger brother Jake or Jason much better, and I felt bad for him. Jake fought his own demons, and his brother's death would surely make the battle more difficult.

I threw myself back into my work and listened for any developments or information about Neil Stonechild's death. I considered his death to be very unusual given his age and the location where his body was found. I trusted the investigation was in good hands.

I dealt with my calls and arrests, and the shift progressed normally. It was my practice to park my patrol car and walk the beat on 20th Street when I was between dispatches. I went to an arcade located at 20th Street West and Avenue G South, where I suspected drug trafficking was taking place. Some local toughs and young offenders hung out there, and I liked to make contacts or arrests there to keep things in line as much as possible. I walked in, let my eyes adjust to the dimness, and began to look over the patrons through the clouds of cigarette smoke. It was a small place, barely up to any building safety codes, with buzzing machines and bustling with young people. I saw Jake in a corner.

Jake came up to me and told me he was out on a temporary absence from a local youth detention facility. He was serving time for one offence or another—I did not ask him because I liked him and it didn't really matter either way. He asked if I'd heard about his brother Neil. I told him I had heard where and how he was found but did not know much more than that. Jake asked me to step off to the side, away from the other patrons. He then told me he had heard on the streets that two brothers had killed his brother and some girl whose name started with the letter P was there. His brother Neil had been at a party in the north end and had gotten very loaded. He had been beaten, thrown into the trunk of a car, and dumped. Jake then asked if I could call his mom, Stella, because she really wanted some answers. I told him I would. Given our location, I felt I could not safely question him any further because the stigma of being seen talking to a police officer could pose a very real threat to Jake. After making it look like I was conducting a street check on him, Jake and I parted company.

I walked back to my patrol car and immediately made notes of what he had told me. It was close the end of my shift, but I was pumped. Nothing offends me more than murder. If what Jake had said was true, this information could break the investigation of Neil Stonechild's death wide open and possibly give some closure to his family. All the persons involved were either young adults or young offenders, and all of them were known to the police. Sadly, they were all First Nations and Métis.

I told a couple of officers in the locker room, but no one knew what I was talking about as Neil Stonechild's death had happened on our days off and the one short newspaper article had attracted little attention. It's one of the perils of the police world—you can easily get information overload. There's always so much going on, an individual officer has trouble keeping track of things they are not directly involved in.

The relationship I had with some detectives was already strained, so I did not want to take this information to them until I knew more about the investigation. Some of the detectives made it a habit to demean uniformed officers and their efforts to assist investigators with their cases. I don't know if it was arrogance or a sense of entitlement or a combination of both. If you paid the proper deference to them and if they saw you as somebody who understood how important they were, then they would deal with you. Making sure you knew your place was more important to them than working co-operatively. These types of attitudes have hurt police forces since the beginning of organized policing. Arrogance can serve a steep bill at the end of the day.

Shortly after meeting Jake, I went to Central Records. Central Records is the depository for all reports left by the Saskatoon police service. It is manned by civilians who process every piece of documentation left by the police. The Central Records staff prepares court documents, enters warrants, and so much more. Without the staff of Central Records Department, our police service would grind to a halt.

I found the file number for the investigation of the death of Neil Stonechild on our local computer system. I asked the file clerk to retrieve the hardcopy for me. I felt like a thief because I had nothing to do with the investigation officially, but I did not want to go to the detectives unprepared and give them information they already had.

The file clerk brought me the file. I read the first few pages, then photocopied it so I could read it all later. I was glad nobody saw me except the clerk because by this time in my service I wasn't exactly sure who the "Friendlies" were anymore. I put the file into my metal clipboard and went back out onto the streets. Once I was back in my patrol car, I let the dispatcher know I was available for calls so I would not be questioned about why I was booked down at the station for long periods of time. In the early 1990s and still today, uniformed members had to account for their time and were subject to much more scrutiny than plainclothes investigators.

One of the reasons for the bad blood between some of the detectives and me was that I had reopened files they had concluded, investigated them, and laid charges. I had been sworn at, undermined, and turned in to my supervisors when these things happened. It did not deter me, it just made me wary.

There were a lot of things causing me concern in 1990 and 1991. The chasm between the new way of policing and the old way was widening. The days where longevity was the only required criteria for someone to become an investigator were becoming numbered, and whether they liked it or not, the days where they would only work with other white men were gone. It was the pain of each step and how long it took to make that concerned me, and I wondered if I would be there at the end of it all.

Once I was in my district, I pulled over and began to read the file in detail. I was shocked to see that the file had been concluded. The investigator's conclusion that Neil Stonechild had wandered up to the North Industrial Area to turn himself in at the Adult Correctional Centre was ludicrous. I had seen things written off during investigations before that raised my eyebrows, but nothing as serious as the death of a seventeen year old in suspicious circumstances.

I called Stella, Neil Stonechild's mother, and arranged to meet her. When I went to her home in the Confederation area of Saskatoon, I was greeted by a cordial and dignified woman. Her pain and frustration were obvious. A mother's grief is one of the strongest emotions. Some of Neil's siblings were there, and while they listened, they did not interrupt. It was clear that Stella was the leader of family. Stella told me basically what Jake had told me, but she gave me more background information on Neil. It was all third-party information. The legal term is hearsay, but I felt it gave investigative direction.

When Stella began to speak about how she and her family were being treated by the police, I didn't know what to say to her. This woman and her family wanted to be treated with respect and kept informed on the progress of the investigation. They'd received at best the barest minimum of consideration a police officer could give without getting himself fired. I could not understand why this had happened to them. I wondered what they thought of me, a uniformed officer who was not part of the investigation, coming to their home. I wanted to help and hopefully get some answers for the family. I also did not want to give them false hope. I have never forgotten the poise and dignity of Neil's mother. Her love for her family was unconditional. I told her I would do whatever I could.

I went to my staff sergeant and told him that I had information regarding the death of Neil Stonechild. He changed my duty hours so that I could have a meeting with the staff sergeant in charge of the Major Crimes and Morality sections. I was on night shift, and my normal hours were 7 p.m. to 7 a.m. The staff sergeant arranged for me to come to work at four o'clock in the afternoon before the plainclothes officers were done shift.

I came to work and steeled myself for the coming meeting. This was one time when the discipline I acquired in the army was working against me. I knew I had to defer to their rank and experience when I spoke to them. I wrote down my concerns in my notebook in point form. Most of my concerns had been raised by reading the file, and meeting with Stella added several more.

A junior uniformed officer was never warmly welcomed in the offices of the plainclothes investigators. There were none of the cordial greetings you would normally receive from coworkers. No "How are you doing? How's the job going?" or anything other than cold stares and that glad-you're-not-talking-to-me look.

I went upstairs and, as I expected, was greeted coldly. I spoke with the staff sergeant and tried to outline my concerns about the investigation for approximately five minutes. The staff sergeant did not crack a notebook and listened only long enough to give me the distinct feeling that he wanted no part of this. He told me I would have to speak to the assigned investigator, Sergeant Jarvis.

It went badly from the first words I spoke. I could tell his temper was up the moment he saw me darken his door. I was told the file was closed. The information I had was hearsay, and I was meddling in things I did not understand.

There is nothing I can recall from that meeting that was even remotely positive. My place in the food chain was made very clear to me. I do not like to use the word racist. I tried to avoid it or bully my way through those types of attitudes with work ethic and reason. I came out of his office forty-five minutes later shaking. I was so full of anger and frustration. He had implied that my meddling could be dealt with in many different ways. My future wife was seven months pregnant at the time and I had a lot to lose. I could only console myself with the thought that what is said is said and there was no way they could not at least revisit the investigation, do at least a little bit of digging, and give Neil Stonechild's death a second look.

I stayed angry for many years, though I didn't realize how angry I was until years later when I testified at the Stonechild Inquiry.

I went back on the street to work my night shift. As always happens, events conspired to force me to get my head back into the job of policing. There was a car chase with a stolen car that started in the Riversdale neighbourhood of Saskatoon and ended with the car crashing by the Victoria Bridge. The passenger bailed out and ran. I arrested the driver at gunpoint. I was still a police officer.

I called Stella when I returned to the day shift. I felt more in peril now and worried that meeting her would land me in serious trouble.

When we met, I told her that the information she had given to me had been passed on to the investigator. I did not tell her what a complete disaster the meeting had been. I hoped against hope that the conversation in the office of the plainclothes investigators had prompted somebody to do something. The following shift, I contacted Stella again, and when I went to her house, she told me that she had not been contacted by anyone.

We both took to criticizing what had or had not happened as far as the Saskatoon police were concerned. I made heated comments along the lines that if Neil Stonechild had been a white youth, more would have been done. I felt the sting and anger of the indifference being shown to Stella and her family. It made me question the motives behind the disregarding of this family's grief. I told Stella there was not a lot more I could do.

I didn't realize at the time the stress this frustration was causing. My wife was almost ready to give birth when I noticed a bald spot on my head the size of a large coin. I thought I had brain cancer. I went to the doctor and was told it was a skin condition called alopecia, caused by stress.

Stella, God bless her, went to the local paper, and an extremely well-written article appeared on the front page detailing the death of Neil Stonechild and the treatment the family had received from the Saskatoon Police Service. Unfortunately, the article included some of the things I had said to her. I was quoted as a senior officer with the Saskatoon police. I was mortified. That evening on the news and in the follow-up articles in the paper, the information officer, holding a hefty file, told members of the media that a tremendous amount of work had gone into investigating Neil Stonechild's death. The chief of police and administration took the same stance. If I felt in peril before, now I felt in jeopardy.

My first son was born a couple of days later. I tried to tell my wife about everything that had happened so far, but a new baby trumps the goings-on at work. I felt isolated and very much on my own. I had given the Stonechild family false hope. I called Stella for the last time and told her she would have to deal with the investigators from here on in.

Still, the day-to-day, night-to-night dispatches and crimes in the life of the patrol officer did not stop because of what had transpired. I waited to be called in and questioned. I became swept up and seized with trying to right other wrongs. I had a harder attitude now and contempt for anyone who did not do their job. I waited and waited to be called in and dealt with for violating policy and interfering with another officer's investigation.

Nothing happened. It was like none of this had ever happened at all.

In 1991, the CBC produced a docudrama about the killing of Helen Betty Osborne in The Pas, Manitoba. I was asked to take a CBC reporter on a ride-along so she could get a perspective on the relationship between natives and police in Saskatoon. Every night after that, a segment of the docudrama "Conspiracy of Silence" was shown. They would show a clip of the ride-along on the national news. CNN and headline news also showed the clips. I took the reporter and her cameraman to calls and we dealt with drunken people, alarms, and all the normal goings-on of the night shift. What made it so ironic was that at the time, Neil Stonechild's tragic story had already started. The spotlight on The Pas and its citizens would be turned on the Saskatoon Police Service nine years later.

I very rarely submitted files for investigation after that. I did them myself. I put the Neil Stonechild file in my barracks box and forgot about it, though I never forgot the Stonechilds.

Over the next nine years, I solidified my attitudes and work ethic. I was a very aggressive patrol officer and aspired to nothing else. I did not seek promotion. It was always in the back my mind that someday someone would talk about the death of Neil Stonechild and how he came to be found frozen to death in a field.

On 29 January 2000, the body of Rodney Naistus was found frozen to death in the Southwest Industrial Area of Saskatoon.

On 3 February 2000, the body of Lawrence Wegner was found frozen to death in the area of the Queen Elizabeth Power Plant southwest of the city of Saskatoon.

In February 2000, I came to work and walked into the station to find it enveloped in an atmosphere of tension and anger. Officers were muttering and speaking in low and angry voices. I was told a man named Darrell Night had come forward with an accusation that he had been driven out of town by two officers, dropped off in subzero temperatures, and made to walk back to the city on his own. Mr. Night stated that he'd been dropped off in the same area that Lawrence Wegner's body had been found.

Senior administration was aggressively interviewing the patrol offi-cers who were on duty that night. Mr. Night's accusations were serious, and interviews were, by necessity, harsh and abrupt. Officers whose in-tegrity had never been questioned became defensive. One of the hardest things is to defend yourself from an accusation if you had nothing to do with what you are being accused of. The atmosphere was frantic. There was blood in the water. The media now had the story, and the most tu-multuous period of the Saskatoon Police Service had begun.

Accusations of murder and racism began. I watched as my coworkers began to reel from blow after blow. Morale plummeted. We were called murderers every day and every night. We were spit at, assaulted, and held in contempt. Of course people still called for the police when they needed help, but everything we did had an edge to it.

At this point, allegations were made that police across Western Can-ada, and in Saskatoon in particular, were regularly driving First Nations people out of their neighbourhoods and dropping them on the outskirts as a punitive and expedient way of solving problems. The term "Starlight Tours" was taken from a newspaper story written by a member of the Saskatoon Police Service in the early nineties in what was supposed to be a humorous piece. He wrote a story about dropping off a troublesome man outside of Saskatoon and making him walk back to town to cool off. It was not funny then and is even less now. The Night incident, in my opinion, happened because those officers were not being supervised. They believed they could do what they did because there would be no consequence. How very wrong they were.

The chief called in the RCMP because of the scope and nature of the investigation. Someone mentioned that the Stonechild matter should be revisited, and I just smiled. I went looking for my notes from the time. I was interviewed several times by members of the RCMP task force in regard to all sorts of incidents and people we had checked or arrested in 2000. It was a funny feeling to be interviewed by other police officers about your work. I never felt defensive because I was confident my work as a patrol officer could withstand any scrutiny.

I knew a new investigation into the death of Neil Stonechild was coming, but I didn't know when or who the investigators would be. Eventually, I was contacted by a corporal with the RCMP. We did not meet at the station or at the hotel the RCMP were using as their home base during the investigation. We met in parking lots. I photocopied my notes for him and tried to recall as many details as I could. The corporal asked me questions about other members of Saskatoon Police Service. I answered as honestly as I could. I never once thought police were involved in Neil Stonechild's death, but I was damn sure they never made any effort to find out with any degree of certainty how Neil Stonechild came to be where he died.

The calls kept coming—crimes continued and even increased as the Saskatoon Police Service was under investigation. Uniformed officers took the brunt of the criticism and scorn heaped upon us. Officers were afraid to do their job and afraid to be accused of being racist while doing it. Street gangs gained a strong foothold during this period of uncertainty. Adding to everything else that was going on, a former Saskatoon police officer was elected mayor. Given the tumultuous state of affairs in Saskatoon, a change in command of the Saskatoon Police Service to me seemed inevitable.

The first three casualties were inflicted. The two officers who dropped Darrell Night off by the Queen Elizabeth Power Plant were suspended and eventually charged with unlawful confinement and assault. Those two I had no problem with. But when the Police Commission, composed of the newly elected mayor, two city councilors, and two members of the community, dismissed Chief Scott, it was a shock.

The new chief was from Calgary and came with an entirely different philosophy of policing. Chief Sabo began making sweeping changes, it seemed to me always at the expense of the front line officers. He created many positions for community liaison; unfortunately the manpower always came from Patrol. He did lay out the groundwork, financially and organizationally, for the present Saskatoon Police Service, however telling us how bad we were and how he was going to fix us caused morale to plummet to a new low.

Through it all, we kept working. It struck me that no one really asked me what my opinion was on everything that was going on except my partner at the time. We had candid conversations, but with everyone else, it was if they were afraid of what they would hear. I remember one conversation in the locker room while our shift was coming on in, relieving the previous shift. Everyone looked beaten, and the frustration they felt was palpable. I started by making an analogy to the beaches on D-day, explaining that many of the casualties on the beach occurred to those who lay there and didn't move forward. They were still police officers. People still needed them. They still needed to do their job regardless. I remember there were some catcalls, but the message was sent.

The RCMP announced that they would not be reopening the Stonechild investigation until the initial investigations into Darrell Night's allegations and the deaths of Rodney Naistus, Lawrence Wegner, and Lloyd Dustyhorn were completed. After the officers who dropped off Darrell Night were convicted, the RCMP announced that Neil Stonechild's body would be exhumed.

The investigation of Neil Stonechild's death was emerging as the most serious allegation against the Saskatoon Police Service. I hoped a new autopsy would yield enough evidence to move the renewed investigation forward. There were so many forces in play by this time, I was struggling to keep up. There were calls for sweeping and all-encompassing inquests into the relationship between the Saskatoon Police Service and the Aboriginal communities.

In the early part of 2002, I testified at the coroner's inquest into the death of Lawrence Wegner. Another officer and I had gone to his apartment to investigate a domestic dispute between Lawrence Wegner's roommate and the roommate's girlfriend the day before he was found dead. The lawyer for the Wegner family was very aggressive, and his disdain for the police was very much in the forefront of his cross-examination.

I remembered the call. I didn't know Lawrence Wegner, and he was not the subject of the call. All I could recall of him was that he was a nervous man, reluctant to speak to the police about what was going on in the apartment. I remember getting off the stand and realizing that the tone set in the courtroom room would be the template for inquests to come. Yet no one from our administration or police association ever asked me about it. As a leader or a union rep, I would have been curious. It reminded me of the marked man scenario from basic training. You felt you were on our own. I am sure other officers felt the same.

In February 2003, the Saskatchewan Minister of Justice announced an inquiry into the death of Neil Stonechild. I knew an already ugly and difficult situation was about to get even uglier and more difficult. I knew I would be in the thick of it, and people would be hurt and reputations ruined.

I don't know where I heard it from, but I heard that the Stonechild report had been purged from the Saskatoon police records as part of a routine purging to free up space in our building. Throughout all the events and the stressful atmosphere, my copy of the report lay forgotten at the bottom of my barracks box in the basement of my home. It was the only copy of the report in existence.

My partner at the time had been designated a sniper with the Emergency Response team. I was happy for and proud of him. I told him I had some sniper material from my time in the service, and I would dig around my barracks box and bring it. A barracks box is basically an army-issued trunk for you to keep your kit in when deployed. I went downstairs and was rummaging through newspaper clippings and different paraphernalia from the army. Old leave passes, evaluations, and copies of old search warrants were scattered inside.

I found the report. I knew instinctively my life would change. My family would be affected. The police service would suffer. Individual reputations would be ruined. So many different people and organizations would read it and spin it whatever way it suited them.

I had been stressed trying to articulate what my concerns were 1991. Now that I had the report in my hands, my concerns were there for everyone to see.

I brought the report upstairs. My wife, who knew a lot more than I thought about the stress I was feeling trying to give as much information as I could to the RCMP about my concerns from 1991, knew right away what I had in my hands. I contacted the RCMP investigator and our deputy chief and told them that I had found the report. I brought it down to the station. I remember thinking that I would be in trouble again because I had clearly violated policy by removing a report from the station. But I did know for certain now that the investigation would be in the spotlight, and the light would not be kind.

The next couple of months were a blur. I stayed on the streets and kept doing the job of policing. Taking calls, and taking abuse related to the unfolding events in Saskatoon policing, was not easy during this period. People didn't care who you were; all they saw was the uniform. What they heard or were told was that we were dangerous and racist. It is a tribute to the young officers—and invariably they are young officers who populate the front line of Patrol—who maintained their professionalism and worked throughout this period. Most of them did not even know who Staff Sergeant Jarvis, Chief Penkala, and Neil Stonechild were.

There were calls for the RCMP to take over policing in Saskatoon, lock, stock and barrel. There were calls for the dissolution of the Saskatoon Police Service as an entity. Not to put too fine a point on it, but four-hundred-plus people could have lost their jobs. I had four children and no other skills other than the army and policing, so the fear was real. On top of this, I had violated policy by keeping a report at my home.

Being charged with a *Police Act* discipline offence is an easy prospect in a profession where everything you do is scrutinized. The tension I felt was compounded by undiagnosed post-traumatic stress from the chase in 1999 and all the other things I had seen. I cannot believe my family and friends put up with me. So many battles are personal in people's lives, and the main reason they are personal is because the embattled do not share with people when the battle is occurring.

I do not know if I ever shared the angst I felt about Neil Stonechild's death with anyone. He was seventeen when he died. I was seventeen when I joined the army. I could relate to the promise seventeen held, and how easily at that age Neil's fate could have been mine, and my mother's anguish if it had. I was working on the railway, drinking and partying all over Northern Ontario, with my fate in the hands of strangers. There would I have gone but for the grace of God.

The indifference shown to his family angered me. Still, I loved being a police officer. I respected and admired most of the people I worked with. These mixed feelings and the nagging suspicion the senior administration had been willfully blind to the distress and grief of the Stonechild family made the following months like walking through the smoke of a forest fire.

I became wary of all the hype and politics surrounding events of 2000 to 2004. I did not want to become anyone's pawn. As a consequence, I guarded my thoughts and beliefs. I just wanted to get through it all.

In October 2003, I was called to testify at the Stonechild Inquiry. It had started in September and was moving forward in fits and starts, disrupted by adjournments, objections, and requests for standing. I remember putting on my dress uniform the morning I was going to testify. I was and still am proud of the uniform. I knew that the next couple of days would be long, and I hoped I would not get flustered or off track.

This part of the inquiry was held on the top floor of the Sheraton Cavalier Hotel in Saskatoon, in what had once been a nightclub called the Top of the Inn. I knew there would be no dancing or music this time.

The room was full of people, family, activists, media, and endless lawyers. Justice Wright sat on a raised stage. My place was to his left. I was sworn in, and the justice told me to sit down. I looked at Stella, and she stared back coldly. I realized that she did not recognize me. My wife, who had come with me, said Stella did not remember me until I started to testify.

The emotion and frustration I felt in 1990 and 1991 came flooding back.

The rules of evidence are different at inquiries. They are far less stringent than at criminal trials. There was a lot of latitude. The questions were a lot more pointed, and you could give your opinion. I definitely was not accustomed to having the freedom to say what I needed to say.

The first lawyer was lead counsel for the inquiry. He led me through my involvement, extracting what I could remember, introducing my notes, the report, and its discovery. I tried to stay as focused as possible. There were many distractions as I was testifying. Reporters were getting up and leaving, family members commenting, and lawyers making notes.

The lead counsel asked pointed and difficult questions. Did I think racism played a part in investigation of Neil Stonechild's death? My answer was racism, indifference, or apathy—the commissioner would have to pick the adjective. He pressed, and my answer was ultimately yes.

I don't even like the word racist. It has been devalued and bantered around by people with specific agendas. It has been used as a weapon to accomplish set goals. The murder of Helen Betty Osborne and its cover-up was racism. Police street-checking native gang members who exploit their own people and call themselves the Native Syndicate or Indian Posse is not. We need to be mindful and not water down what is truly racist by using the term every time somebody does something we don't agree with. Racism is, in and of itself, an ugly, vile practice. Its practitioners are weak and simple, and likely small in number. It is not confined to any particular race either. I know Indians who hate white people with a passion, and vice versa. Racism is the defence or excuse of the ignorant and uninspired. It is so easy to hate, to blame, to deflect when people are different from you.

I testified for the entire afternoon. I was cross-examined by lawyers representing the police association, Constables Hartwig and Senger, and the Saskatoon Police Service. My testimony soundly criticized the Saskatoon Police Service of the late 1980s and early 1990s and its investigations. I also testified about the improvements I had seen over the years.

As we were going to adjourn for the day, the lawyer representing Staff Sergeant Jarvis indicated that he wanted to be the last one on the second day to cross-examine me in light of my testimony on the first day. He looked angry and pugilistic. I suspected the second day of testimony would be a long one.

The next morning, the first lawyer to cross-examine me was Don Worme. He represented Stella and the Stonechild family. I have always admired him. An articulate, intelligent, and passionate man, he started slowly. He complimented me on my uniform, my service with the military, and my dedication. I respected him before the inquiry and respected him more when it was over. He was the only other native person I spoke to involved in the Stonechild Inquiry. We were on different paths looking for the same justice. He clarified one part of my testimony where I had named families as being involved in criminal activities. I was glad he gave me the opportunity to say that not all members of the named families were criminals.

The lawyer for the Federation of Saskatchewan Indian Nations (FSIN), Sy Halyk, one of the most prominent lawyers in Saskatchewan, was next. I had been before him on some criminal trials, and I knew he was very skillful at cross-examination. Smooth and reassuring when he spoke, he could also be ruthless when seeking the truth. He started out by thanking me for keeping a copy of the Stonechild report. Someone told me early in my police career to be wary of any lawyer who compliments you at the start of your testimony. By day two, wary had gone out the window, and I was all in.

Mr. Stevenson, the counsel for Staff Sergeant Jarvis, was the last lawyer to cross-examine me. He came out swinging. Given his client's situation, I would have done the same. He did his best to discredit me and to make Jarvis's investigation look thorough and exhaustive. I had never dealt with him in court before. He touched on what was a raw nerve for me. He point-blank asked why I didn't do more in 1991 to move the Stonechild investigation forward. I could not explain the jeopardy I felt in 1991. I could not bring myself to say there were times where I trusted the criminals more than some of the detectives in the Saskatoon Police Service in 1991. I could not bring myself to say that I felt safer on the streets than in the police station. It was how I felt, but I couldn't bring myself to say it. As he pressed me to concede that I didn't have investigative experience and didn't know what a good investigation was, I began to get angry. Anger on the stand is self-defeating, and I did my best to control it. I knew Mr. Stevenson was doing his job and doing his best to salvage Jarvis's reputation, but was an ugly and unfortunate way to finish my testimony. I was excused and got off the stand exhausted.

As I walked out of the room, I took a last look at Stella and her family and wondered what the coming days would bring them.

My staff cap under my arm, I met my wife at the entrance. We took the elevator downstairs, and as we were exiting the lobby, a man who had publicly tried to implicate me in the freezing death of Lawrence Wegner said to me, "Maybe you're not so bad after all."

I looked directly at him, said, "Fuck you. Once you fire a shot, you can't get it back," and walked away. I think that summed up how I felt at the time.

A reporter came up to my wife and me and asked if he could interview me for a book he was writing about Neil Stonechild. I took his card and kept going.

I had no idea what reception awaited me when I went back to work. The chief asked me to come to his office once I was back at station. I had mixed feelings going to the chief. I didn't want to be told "Good job!" I didn't know what to think. The chief was cordial and thanked me for my candour and told me not to worry about anything.

We left and went home. When we got home, the phone would not stop ringing. Officers were calling and thanking me for my testimony. One sergeant dropped by my house and asked me if I was all right. These are the police I know and love. The truth, or as close as we can get to it, is the goal of all good police officers.

I still cannot help thinking about how other police officers felt in the period of 2000 to 2005. Many of them were paying for sins they had not committed. I admired them for it. They kept going out day after day, night after night, taking abuse and doing the job they had sworn to do without fear or favour.

You always wonder if you made a difference. It's the nature of the beast. Until I started writing this, I never knew how I felt.

I never wanted to be bitter or point fingers. I just wanted to tell my story and let it speak for itself. Like all things, people will take what they want and spin it whatever way suits them. It is human nature. Even the best person thinks, "How will this affect *me*?" You cannot help it.

So much pain, and to what end?

The inquiry continued—more witnesses, more controversy, and more accusations—until it wrapped up months later. I returned to shift a couple days after testifying, and it was like nothing happened. The only incident was once when I got on the elevator, some senior detectives got off so they would not have to ride with me. I had expected worse.

Shortly after I testified in October 2003, a young off-duty security guard was murdered in broad daylight in front of the Midtown mall. I was one of the first officers at the scene. I knew from the location and nature of the wound that his wound was mortal. The killer, a young offender, was arrested trying to flee the downtown area. The tragedy was a signal to us all: Enough madness! We still have to live together. It was time to move forward.

On October 26, 2004, the province released the final report of the Stonechild Inquiry. My wife and I were watching the local news when Justice Wright's findings were read. We were shocked. The justice concluded that two Saskatoon police constables had Neil Stonechild in their custody the night he died. The hue and cry for their heads began. The frenzy was renewed.

Through the entire furor, most people missed the important findings and recommendations made by the justice. Most people missed the self-initiated changes made not only by the Saskatoon Police Service but by police services all across Canada. Accountability and transparency in policing became inescapable commitments. The changes had already started when this inquiry and other inquiries across Canada accelerated the process.

For the most part, I am confident that a case like Neil Stonechild's cannot happen again. I think other organizations have learned as well. I think the media will be more fair, and more investigative work will be done before editors let reporters blaze short, attention-grabbing headlines which ultimately flounder under scrutiny. There are some excellent journalists out there who must have shaken their heads more than once. You have to be brave to be honest, and avoid feeding the base needs of sensationalism. Just tell the story—it's compelling of its own accord.

The groups representing native people will not water down the significance of a death like Neil Stonechild's by opening hotlines to elicit as many complaints as they can. They bogged down and dissipated the impact of something demanding their full effort and attention.

The vice chief of the FSIN went so far as to call native officers with Saskatchewan police forces mere tokens when he demanded the First

Nations be allowed to form their own police forces. Divisive rhetoric did nothing to help our people come to terms with how they felt about what was going on.

Most of the reasonable voices were drowned out in the native community by the headline grabbers. I think we did ourselves a disservice by allowing this. It was clear that an injustice had taken place, and we were in a strong position to ask for it to be righted. Not only native leaders but all politicians I hope have learned to proceed slowly and do what needs to be done and wait for the results. In all of this lies true leadership. We all deserve it, and we all need it.

The hysteria and emotion of that whole 2000–2005 period revealed how thin the crust of fairness is when people see tragedy as opportunity. I've seen this many times in my career. The whole process should have been dignified and sober. An unbiased and impartial search for the truth should have been the goal of our leaders. Somehow, though, through all the finger-pointing, accusations, and malice, we came away with a better police service and hopefully a better province with stronger leaders.

This is Neil Stonechild's legacy. A young man who died under still unexplained circumstances made us look at ourselves in a different light. His death made us examine how we do things, what our attitudes really are, and how we will conduct ourselves in the future. Although it is no compensation to his family in their grief and pain, it is a strong legacy.

I had expected the report to soundly criticize the Saskatoon Police Service for its failure to properly investigate the death of Neil Stonechild and the 1991 leadership for failing to ensure a proper investigation was done. I never expected the report would make the finding that the police constables had Neil Stonechild in custody the night he died. There were just too many unanswered questions. If we had done our job the way we were supposed to in 1991, maybe we would have had those answers.

When I returned to work, the atmosphere was grim. Everyone was angry and frustrated. It was inevitable that the chief would have to act on the findings. I felt a kind of emotional numbness. It was like I had nothing left in the tank. But the business of policing continued, and I went back onto the streets.

Less than a month later, the two constables were fired. They had never been charged with anything.

In May 2005, I testified at an arbitration hearing held to determine if the firing of the two constables was justified. The counsel for the police commission was a prominent lawyer from Prince Albert. He had an aggressive cross-examination style, and we had a heated exchange when he accused me of deliberately hiding the Stonechild report. I was furious— where did that come from? If he had any idea how I felt about all of this tragedy, he would have never asked the question. I was so angry, I told him that if I had ever made an accusation like that without foundation, I would be ashamed, and he should be as well. The arbitrator told us both to calm down. I got off the stand still angry and wondered what was next.

Shortly afterwards, a book was published called *Starlight Tours*. There was talk of a movie.

The fired constables appealed all the way to the Supreme Court of Canada but remained fired.

I wrote my sergeant's exam and was promoted to sergeant in 2007. I've been a patrol sergeant ever since, on the same streets I have policed my entire career.

So is the Neil Stonechild story over? Sadly, no, it will never be over. There are too many unanswered questions. There are theories and speculations about what happened to Neil Stonechild, but no solid proof of anything.

In February of 2004, a round dance was held at a community centre in Saskatoon. One of the organizers turned away a native man who had been drinking too much. The man wandered into the cold night and was found dead from hypothermia shortly after. A thorough investigation proved it was death by misadventure.

If the death of Neil Stonechild had been investigated with some honour and purpose, who knows what the outcome would have been for us all? The truth is the thin crust on which justice walks. If we created an injustice to right an injustice then there has been no justice at all.

17.

Late Nights on the Streets

There are times on night shifts when you're so tired it is hard to even talk. For years, the biggest gap in police coverage in the city of Saskatoon (and probably every other jurisdiction) was between midnight and 6 a.m. Yet it was during those hours we had some of our busiest nights. The normal call load of domestics, accidents, and assaults could quickly tie up a platoon's manpower. Throw in robberies, break-ins, and in-progress crimes, and soon all your officers are committed to something and unavailable to respond to emergencies. For most of my career with the Saskatoon Police Service, the crime rate in Saskatoon was the highest in Canada. There were many nights when we were stretched to the limit, and that is when a murder or fatal accident would occur.

When I first started off as patrol constable, those kinds of nights were exciting and a twelve-hour shift could go by in a flash. I loved nights, and I still do after twenty-eight years. They are full of anticipation, full of danger, and totally addictive. After a few years in, I started to wonder where the hell all the other cops were. Once I was promoted to sergeant, I really began to wonder where the hell all the other cops were.

The truth of it is that they were at home sleeping because they were not in the Patrol division.

I had been with the Saskatoon Police Service for about a year. It was night shift. The staff sergeant read the duty roster and announced who was paired up with whom. I was the odd man out. I was supposed to pair up with a sergeant at 11 p.m. I knew right off the top it would be a night-killer.

Most patrol sergeants in 1989 were not dynamic. The sergeant I was paired up with was a quiet guy at the best times. A gentle soul, he was a career police officer who had numerous children and was putting them all through university. Policing to him was a job. Eleven p.m. rolled around and I was stopping cars and checking people, trying to avoid pairing up. I think the sergeant was good with this because he didn't call me on the radio to remind me that we were partners.

It was around 1 a.m. when I saw taillights in an alley.

I pulled into the alley to check out the car and its occupants. I hit the overhead lights and got out. It took me a couple of seconds to realize what I was seeing. A male had a knife, and a pregnant woman bound with rope was on the front seat beside him. I cannot remember what I said on the radio. I pulled my gun and told him to get out of the car. The woman was terror-stricken. Her eyes were wide and full of fear.

The male got out with the knife still in his hand. He was muscular and had the cold eyes of a shark. I yelled for him to drop the knife or I would shoot him. The patrol wagon pulled into the alley, and he threw the knife aside. We took him into custody. The woman, a prostitute, was untied and taken to hospital. I learned later that pregnant prostitutes were hot commodities in the sex trade. I laid charges of kidnapping and sexual assault with a weapon on the male.

The next morning, a local radio station that featured a call-in segment called "Boots and Salutes" carried the story. I got saluted all morning. Apparently this male was a suspect in a string of violent sexual assaults. He always picked his victims carefully. They were always native, prostitutes, and undervalued. He was confident no one would charge him, much less testify against him.

He went to court in the morning and was remanded to the correctional centre. He had a "show cause" hearing the next day. A show cause hearing is a hearing where the Crown has to show the court why an accused should be held in custody prior to his trial. It is also the defence lawyer's opportunity to show the court why the accused should be released. The defence lawyer made an impassioned plea for his client, saying that the suspect had been beaten at the jail by other inmates because of the nature of the accusations against him. He was released from custody on an undertaking with strict conditions.

When I returned to work, my inspector told me that I was paired up with a senior officer and we would be in plainclothes. Our task would be to do surveillance on the newly released suspect to ensure he was complying with his bail conditions.

He never left his house. We went to lunch at a local Greek restaurant.

We learned that our waitress was the suspect's girlfriend. Saskatoon can be a small town sometimes. I told her about her boyfriend and how I believed he was sexual sadist who preyed on native women. She weakly defended him. My partner said I gave her too much information. I did not agree. I wanted her to tell the suspect how much we knew. If it prevented one more attack, for me it was mission accomplished.

The trial date was set, and my victim was nowhere to be found. Later in my career, I began to request subpoenas for my own cases, and I would track them down and serve my witnesses. Back then, I did not have the experience and worked with the existing systems. The charges against my suspect were stayed, and he promptly moved out of the province.

I never knew my victim's story, where she was from, or why she felt compelled to work the streets as a prostitute while she was pregnant. I was too busy thinking that I was a hero for saving her, and I did not do my job the way I should have.

The suspect moved back to Saskatoon a few years ago. He is quiet, broken even, and never too far out of my mind.

No detectives were involved in this case. In the present Saskatoon Police Service, detectives from the Sex Crimes unit would have been called out to finish the investigation. Back then, apparently that wasn't how we did business, and we can only speculate on the reasons why.

Night shifts are often the determining factor in most police officers' careers when it comes to longevity in the Patrol division. I think we all know night shifts are part of the job when we choose careers as police officers, but the physical reality of night shifts is that they are hard on your body. Just how hard can come as a surprise to some officers. Socially, night shifts can affect the relationships you have with your family and friends. Any shift worker can tell you that we are night people in a day-shift world. Life goes on around you, and you miss a lot of things. My wife raised our four children with me gone two complete nights out of every eight days. Those are the kind of things you don't realize when you choose this trade.

All people who work night shift will get this. There's nothing worse than working a night shift where it's busy and you're short on manpower. You make quick decisions and do your best to maintain order. You and the other people on your shift may have dealt with up to twenty calls each. You might have been at a traumatic event. You are physically and mentally exhausted. Then some person who had enjoyed the comfort and warmth of their bed starts to criticize or second-guess what you have done.

There are two kinds of realities in policing. There's day-shift reality, where everything is ordered and in its place, and there's night-shift reality, where events are fluid and sometimes chaotic. People inhabiting the day-shift reality need to take a moment before they speak, to reflect on what a night-shift worker has done before they start talking. I don't know how many times I would look at an executive officer while they were talking about an overdue file or an unanswered e-mail and think, "Are you for real?"

I am not saying patrol officers on night shift are exempt from criticism or relieved of the responsibilities of everyday police life. But sometimes you've got to give them a couple minutes to switch from the hyper-vigilance mode to normal mode before you start dishing out the gruel. I know from personal experience that nothing will make people disrespect you more. Leaders who are cognizant of the realities of the night shift and remember what it was like to work nights will usually take a couple of minutes before they talk. The constables quickly recognize good leadership and equally as fast know which senior officers to avoid. So as a leader, if you are being avoided, it's time to take a second look at yourself.

I have nothing but the greatest respect for people who work nights. Paramedics, doctors, nurses, firefighters, maintenance people, and anyone else who is up at 3 a.m. doing a job are all part of the brotherhood and sisterhood only a portion of the world knows. There is certain nobility to it. Some do it out of necessity, and some by choice. I chose.

One night in the winter of 2011, a call came in of a stabbing behind an apartment building at one of the busiest intersections in Saskatoon. The man had apparently gone to buy drugs, and dealers robbed him. They cut his throat. One of the constables, a former paramedic who had less than a year's service with the Saskatoon police, pinched the severed artery before the paramedics arrived and kept it closed in the ambulance with the victim, right until she was relieved by a doctor in the emergency room. She saved his life. In the process, her patrol jacket was saturated with blood.

I got to the scene and put crime-scene tape up, which included blocking off the entrance to a very busy 7-11 store. The night was cold and busy. It was a payday, and the alcohol was flowing freely. We had limited manpower, and even though I was the area sergeant, I stayed at the crime scene. The bars closed and an ice fog socked in with the cold temperatures. Like a scene from "The Walking Dead," intoxicated people would walk up to the crime-scene tape, bump into it, and be told that the 7-11 was closed. They would look at me mortified that they could not get to the "Sev" and lurch away into the night. It was the weirdest thing.

Detectives from Major Crimes took over the case and we all went home to sleep before the following night shift. The next evening I was the acting staff sergeant, and the officer who had saved the victim came to me to get a new coat. As it was an after-hours issue, I went down to the quartermaster's stores and gave her a brand-new coat. Then we went on our days off. When I came back, I had an e-mail from the quartermaster wanting to know where the contaminated coat was and why I had issued an entirely new one. Sometimes when you get an e-mail it is best just to go for a walk before you answer. I went for a walk, came back, and sent a reply. I told the quartermaster that no amount of cleaning would ever erase the memory of the trauma from the coat. Every time the officer put her patrol jacket back on, she would be reminded of a high-stress incident.

Sometimes there is a huge disconnect between operational policing and administrative duties.

A woman is detained after a shooting in Saskatoon's north end.
(Courtesy The StarPhoenix)

18.

"We Know"—Who Knew?

I was having a candid conversation with an executive officer, and during the conversation, I remarked on how our relationship was often confrontational. I said that I had little time for most of them and tolerated them only because I had to. Equally frank, the officer said, "We know." We both laughed. Who knew?

Every police officer starts off in Patrol. The importance of a strong and well-trained Patrol division cannot be overemphasized. The raw material of every police department is there. It is also very important to have a well-led Patrol division. My experience has shown me most police departments do not have that, or are just starting to get it.

Except for fifteen months I spent in the Street Crime unit, I have always been a patrolman. It was here my heart was. I loved the feeling of being the watchman and of being able to come to the aid of anyone quickly. When I was at work, I was totally committed to the job at hand. The sense of duty and obligation never diminished over the years, and, ever the hammerhead, I could never understand when others were not as committed.

The attitude of most police services toward patrol officers is like the attitude in the military toward the combat arms: they are a numerous and boorish necessity. For years, going back to Patrol from a plainclothes position was considered a demotion. I was on an executive development course and the instructor used an analogy that failing in a leadership role could mean finding yourself back in Patrol. I took exception and told him so.

For years, no consideration was given to the leadership abilities of patrol sergeants before they were put charge of the youngest and most impressionable police officers. Still, in the present Saskatoon Police Service, there are no tests or competency checks for patrol sergeants before they are assigned to Patrol. I think that as an organization, we miss a golden opportunity to shape the future of the service by not giving constables the best leadership we can.

Nothing gets my dander up more than people—especially police officers—disrespecting patrol officers because they are patrol officers. A lot of police officers forget where they started from after they leave Patrol. Magically, the time they spent in Patrol was without mistakes, and everything they did in Patrol was flawless. Now, because they are investigators or administrators, Patrol is a mess.

I have been told many times in my career that I needed to be a better-rounded police officer. I needed to step up and go into the investigative sections. I would shake my head and think to myself that if you wanted to be a well-rounded police officer, Patrol was going to give you everything you needed and more. If I had gone to the investigative sections, I think I would have had less experience with people as a leader.

I do not disrespect police officers who have taken day shift jobs or have gone into investigative sections. I just want them to not disrespect patrol officers. If they ever did, then it was game on.

I made the conscious decision to stay in Patrol for my entire career. Some of my coworkers just could never get their heads around that. Some of them even said I was abdicating my responsibility as a leader by staying in uniform. I think nothing could be further from the truth. As a senior officer, I think it's important for the other patrol officers to see you in uniform and on the street. It was no secret that I saw the value and importance of their work. I was always very vocal about it.

Around 2000, I was working a day shift and of course was close to the end of my shift when the call came in of a shooting. I was close and started to head there.

I did not have an extendable microphone for the portable radio I had signed out at the start of my shift. The commissioner had been ordered not to issue them because they could not resolve some radio issues and thought the extended microphones might be the problem. The extendable mic is the one you see on most police officers now—it extends from the radio and is attached to their vest or a clip. It allows officers to speak on the radio without having to hold it in their hand. This is a very important officer safety issue—you need your hands to be free.

I rolled up on the call, and as I exited the patrol car, I could see people in a panic streaming out the back door of the apartment building. I drew my pistol and went to the apartment where the shooting had occurred. I could hear a female screaming, anguished screams I had heard too many times before.

I swung the apartment door open and scanned for threats or suspects. I saw a female over a male lying on the kitchen floor. Blood was streaming from his head in spite of her attempts to staunch the flow. I asked where the gun was. She just looked at me, overcome with shock. It is a strange thing to remember, but the apartment was immaculately clean. I felt a twinge of fear, realizing I had probably passed the gunman on the way in. I still had my gun in my hand and was unable to use my radio to tell other officers what was going on. She started to scream, "He shot himself," over and over. Other officers came into the apartment. I could hear the sirens as more and more officers arrived. This is one of those unique sounds, alarming yet comforting when you're the first to arrive at a serious call.

I escorted the female from the apartment and turned her over to an officer outside who would transport her to the detectives. As I stepped into the hallway, I saw half a dozen officers, weapons in hand, and half a dozen radios tossed onto the hallway floor because they could not effectively deploy their weapons and talk on the radio at the same time.

As it turned out, the victim, a well-known criminal, had indeed shot himself in the head. His friend panicked and took the gun before the police arrived. He had passed me as I went into the apartment building. He was thankful I did not recognize him as he had an outstanding warrant at the time.

I left my report after the investigators took over the scene and came home late as usual, with more ghosts for my closet. The next day I came in to start my shift and asked for an extended microphone. The commissioner refused, and my blood shot up. I went to the staff sergeant and told him my story of the radios discarded in the hallway. He replied, "Orders are orders." I then told him in an unsteady but defiant voice that I would not go on the street without the microphone. In essence, I was refusing to work in unsafe conditions. It was a big step as I still had small children and needed this job.

He looked at me incredulous and told me I could be in big trouble. I told him I did not care. A flurry of phone calls between the staff sergeant, duty officer, and ultimately the deputy chief took place. Fully expecting to be suspended, I held my breath. Eventually, the staff sergeant went to the commissioner and told him to issue the microphones, and I went back on the street. I never heard another thing about this, nor was I was ever spoken to about it.

The Saskatoon Police Service had been under the same chief from 1982 until 1991. He was a real old-school chief—in my view, always opposed to change. He toed the line on budgets and even returned money to the city. In 1991, we got a new chief, an ex-RCMP officer who came to the Saskatoon Police to make changes. He had a lot of ideas, and started a big push toward community-based policing.

One of the initiatives was called a community initiative report. We were required to leave a report if we walked through a mall or any of the sorts of things we do in the normal course of our duties. Some guys left hundreds. It was lip service, and I did not participate or leave any community initiative reports despite the constant reminders that it would affect my performance reports.

I was on patrol when I received a message to go see the new chief. I was thrown off—no constables or at least uniformed constables got a one-on-one with the chief unless they were in trouble. I did not know what to think as I went to his third-floor office. I had challenged a lot of people up until that point and had come through none the worse for wear. Maybe it was all coming home to roost now.

The chief told me to come in. Smiling a politician's smile, he called me by my first name. I have never been comfortable with casual interaction between ranking officers and myself. I had too much army in me. It was not until I was my late forties that I would refer to officers by their first name.

The chief spread out a bunch of papers on his desk and began to explain why he had called me in. He explained that other police agencies were creating police liaison officer positions to try to bridge the gap between natives and the police. He told me that I would have the freedom to make the position my own. He asked me to read over the material and to have an answer for him by my next day shift, six days away. I thanked him and said I would have an answer for him when I got back.

I walked out of his office thinking, "What just happened here?" Then I became a little bit offended. Would he have offered this to a white police officer? Was there to be a competition? I do not believe this well-intentioned man intended this to be unfair. I did, however, think that he did not think it all the way through. Would the position have any credibility with other police officers if I were appointed to it because I was native? Would native people respect the position if they knew the officer was not the best officer found after a competition? Would I be seen as a token?

There were still a lot of operational issues, and if I took this job, I would no longer be a street cop. I thought that being on the street in uniform and doing my job was the best form of liaison. A lot of people knew who I was on sight. Even kids would shout and point, "It's Indian Ernie!" I wrestled with all of this for a couple of days. At the appointed time, I went to the boardroom, where the chief and the other executives were seated at a long table. The chief greeted me warmly, "Come in, Ernie, and sit down." He had the look of a man about to announce a public relations triumph. I do not think he or any of the executive officers expected anything other than a "Yes sir, I will do it!" response.

The chief came right to the point. "So, Ernie, have you made your decision?"

Nervous, I replied that I was happy where I was, and that I loved Patrol and was loyal to my platoon. "I do not think I am the man for this position, sir."

His face reddened. I think I had embarrassed him. He was so sure I would buy in. I added that the position should be competed for in fairness to the other officers.

The chief was ex-RCMP and quite obviously not used to union contracts. Redder still, he turned to the executive officers, then to me, and said, "I should have expected this from a young hotshot like you." He turned his back to me, and I became a *persona non gratia*. Someone tersely told me that I was dismissed, and I got up and left. I turned my portable radio back on and headed out to my patrol car.

A couple months later, I was sent to an Aboriginal officers' conference at the RCMP Depot in Regina. It was the first time I had ever heard of such a thing. Aboriginal officers from all over the province were gathered in one place, RCMP and municipal police. I felt honoured to be part of it. It was exciting. I met a lot of great people. One of the guys from the RCMP had been in the PPCLI battle school while I was military police there. He had kept his braid and told me how much he enjoyed policing. Everything was pretty positive until we were all brought to the theatre to be addressed by senior RCMP executive officers.

I walked in and sat down. The officers were on a raised stage at a table. An officer outlined plans for Native Policing Units (NPUs) to be set up on reserves, the idea being that native police officers could live where they worked and be part of the community. It sounded noble, and unrealistic. Policing in any community, whether you are native, white, or any other race, is a difficult and sometimes thankless job. There has to be a separation when you are done work. Putting these officers in 24/7 policing posts was only asking for trouble. There are people who hate the police just for being police. Native people are certainly not immune to this. In many cases, they have more reasons to dislike police than other people in Saskatchewan.

The RCMP has long history with First Nations people; most of it is good, but there were dark times as well. Residential schools were filled with the assistance of the RCMP. To put the officers gathered in the theatre into such high-profile positions without consideration for their well-being seemed wrong.

I got up and said so. Senior RCMP officers were used to being listened to and not questioned about their ideas. The officer who had been talking gave me a stern look and asked what agency I was with—a little intimidation tactic, I felt. I pushed on, saying the RCMP administration was expecting too much from their native officers. Some of the NCOs were giving me the "enough" sign. They still had to work there, and this was their organization.

I told the officers that there were some significant historical parallels to how they were presenting the new plan: white men, senior in rank, with the power to make or break the careers of those who disagreed with them, sitting on a raised stage, dictating what was going to happen in the future without consulting the people on the ground.

I was not making any friends with the senior RCMP administration. I was saying what I thought needed to be said. The officer said that it was not their intent and moved on to other topics. Some RCMP officers said thanks, but most avoided me, as if being seen with me after the exchange would sewer their careers.

That night, we went out for beers in Regina. I was still full of nervous energy from talking in the theatre. I suspected that what I had said would make its way back to Saskatoon Police Service's executive officers. I worried that my talking would be perceived as insubordinate and less than gracious to our hosts. Still, I believed then and still believe that the best way to effect change in the relations with native people and police is to ask the front-line people first.

The next morning, we were back in the theatre. I had no idea what to expect. It was then that I was told that I would be speaking to all of these officers about how I policed. I had had no notice and had prepared nothing—a classic blindside. Mounties are good.

I got up and talked about how I did things. Our chief was there. I talked about getting out of the car and talking to everyone possible. To be seen to care was as important to me as it was to be seen on the street. It was not my best speech, and I would love the opportunity to do it again, but hopefully I got my message across.

After I was promoted to Sergeant, some of the investigators in the Major Crimes section told me that there would be openings in the near future and I should put my name forward. I was conflicted. I loved Patrol and liked to teach. I mulled it over for a couple of weeks, and then I went and saw the staff sergeant in charge of Major Crimes. I went to his office and asked for a couple of minutes of his time. I told him I was interested in coming to his section. He looked at me like I had just fallen off the truck. He told me that he didn't think I had what it took to dedicate myself to a case that might stretch out over a long period of time. He told me I didn't have any investigative experience. He told me I would need to speak to the superintendent.

When I went to the superintendent's office, it was the same thing. He told me I didn't have any investigative experience. He told me nobody comes from Patrol to Major Crimes. He referred me to the inspector in charge of the Criminal Investigations Division. He wasn't at work, and I had to go to a course at the Saskatchewan Police College.

One night he called my cell phone and told me he was very happy I wanted to come to the investigative sections. He told me I would have to start out in break-and-enter section or stolen autos. I told him that if he thought I was going to do penance for him or anyone else in the department he was sadly mistaken and to forget I had even asked about Major Crimes.

I hung up the phone, and initially I was mad, but after a few moments I realized I was responsible in part for their perceptions. I had always been a patrol officer. I was very vocal about how important an effective Patrol section was, and in the end no one could see me as anything else. Fortunately, Patrol is a place I liked to be. So no harm. I cannot speak for the executive officer's reasons for keeping me in patrol. What there was here was a lesson to young constables: If you want to be an investigator at some point in your career, do not paint yourself into a corner. Make your intentions known early and often. Clearly state what your career goals are and pursue them. If you are happy in Patrol, stay happy and enjoy the challenges.

Being mean-spirited or short-tempered when you are a supervisor is about as effective as cavalry charging tanks. Your people will lose respect for you and won't perform to their full potential. A lot of times, all people need is the opportunity to try, or the experience and knowledge you hold as a supervisor to enable them to try.

I think the Saskatoon Police Service has moved away from the old-fashioned paramilitary organization we were in 1987. There are still people in leadership positions who are insecure with their own ability, who can be mean-spirited and petty with junior officers. It is the responsibility of other leaders to correct and rein in this type of supervision as soon as they see it.

I volunteered to be part of the implementation and instructor cadre for a new computer system. I was totally out of my comfort zone, and the training occupied a lot of my time. It was a good lesson for me. It showed me how close to being inflexible I had become. One day when we were training a group of NCOs on the new system for managing files and investigations, we were all in the lobby outside the classroom having coffee during a break. The NCOs were talking about their constables' shortcomings and mistakes. It was an animated discussion. I held my hand up and looked at my peers and said, "What do you think our sergeants used to say about us twenty years ago?"

Shortly after I was promoted to sergeant in 2006, I was entitled to more time off because of my seniority. It seemed like I was accumulating more than I was using. So I started to take the first couple hours off on every day shift. Quite frankly, it helped me to use up some time, but it also helped me to avoid the bane of my existence: morning meetings. One morning, I came in and went for my usual run. I had just gotten off the treadmill when one of my constables told me that she had brought in an arrest from a domestic, and when she was giving him his call to his lawyer, he began to fight with her. The special constable in detention was a new guy. He did not help her.

I was livid. I showered quickly and changed into my uniform. I was going up to detention to talk to this kid, and it was not going to be good.

I went for a walk around the station first. I then went to detention area, where the special constable looked like he was going to faint when he saw me. I asked point-blank if he had ever been in a fight. When he replied no, I asked him, "Not even in the schoolyard or with a sibling?" He replied no. I couldn't believe it, but I realize now that there are people we are hiring who have never been in a fight or seen violence other than on television.

I wasn't as angry anymore. I told him he was allowed one "shock and awe," but the next time an officer needed assistance, he'd better be in there and fully committed.

There are eight special constables in the detention area of the Saskatoon police station. A male and female officer are assigned to each shift. Usually they are young and waiting for a chance to go to the police college to train as regular constables. These eight special constables can process thousands of arrests each year. Along with the sergeant in charge of detention, they are responsible for the health and well-being of arrested persons. They must manage, track, and record all of the arrested persons' property, and top it all off with the requirement for properly completed paperwork. There are no windows in detention, and working there is equivalent to working in a tunnel. Most of the special constables who do their time in detention usually make for above-average police officers once they come out of police college.

Sometimes you just have to chuckle at life. (Courtesy Saskatoon Police Service)

19.

Thinking on Your Feet

Around 1992, on a day shift, two other constables and I responded to a call of a suicidal female threatening to hang herself from her third-floor balcony at an apartment in the west end. When we arrived, the woman was standing outside the rails of her balcony with one end of a sheet tied around her neck and the other tied to the railings.

An officer on the ground began talking to her. She was yelling at him not to try to stop her. I got into the apartment building and made my way to her apartment door. I could hear her yelling at the officer on the ground. Another officer had crawled up on the second-floor balcony directly underneath her. Her door was unlocked, and I slowly entered her apartment. I was trying to sneak up and pull her back over the rail. I got to the patio door when she saw me and jumped.

The officer on the second floor balcony reached with one hand, grabbed the sheet, and with his other hand used a knife to cut it, simultaneously pulling her onto the second-floor balcony. I made it to the rail to see this and would not have believed it possible. It was the bravest, best-timed act I had ever seen.

She was taken to the hospital, and when I drove back to the station, I told my sergeant what had happened. The original constable on the ground confirmed the story, and the quick-thinking constable, who was my regular partner at the time, was nominated for the Chief's Award.

The very next night, we were having coffee in a restaurant when a woman began to choke. The same officer got up, did the Heimlich manoeuvre, and saved her. I was in awe.

It was close to the end of a shift in 2007 when we responded to a call of a male who had been stabbed. It was during rush hour, and getting through the heavy traffic was difficult. I arrived at the same time as a constable and his recruit, who was still in training. We saw a male stabbed, lying in front of the steps leading to the front door of the residence. We drew our weapons and started to deploy. An ambulance had arrived and was staging back. With no thought for his personal safety, the constable crouched down and, weapon pointed toward the threat, went to the injured man. He pulled him backwards toward the waiting ambulance, all the while keeping his gun trained on the door of the house.

Those are the kind of constables I work with. They teach me humility and remind me of the responsibility we have as leaders to ensure they always have the proper equipment and training.

It was a Sunday night shift, February 2012. I was acting as staff sergeant. The night for the most part had been uneventful. I had had enough of the office and had taken a patrol car out to take a look around. The temperature was −10°C, and it was one of those winter nights when hoarfrost was on the trees and steam was rising from the river. Saskatoon is a beautiful city in the winter at night.

Just before 2 a.m., a call came in. An intoxicated woman was walking in the traffic lanes of the Broadway Bridge. Another sergeant and I volunteered for the call. I pulled off of 19th Street and started up the Broadway Bridge. I could see the taillights of a patrol car turning onto Broadway Avenue. The other sergeant radioed that he did not see the woman on the roadway and was going to check the area. I was halfway up the bridge when I felt more than saw the woman. She was seated on the west railing, her feet dangling over the edge. I stopped my patrol car and radioed that the woman was on the bridge.

I quietly got out of my car. The woman was rocking back and forth and crying, deep, heart-wrenching sobs. She took off her jacket and let it fall to the sidewalk. She made motions with her hands to push off. I walked toward her slowly and said, "The river is cold, girl. Come off of there."

She turned and looked at me briefly and said, "No, no, no." The brief second she looked at me made my heart sink. She looked just like my daughter—hairstyle, gothic clothing and makeup. I almost froze in place. There was a jersey barrier separating the sidewalk from the roadway, and I knew going over the barrier would be too sudden a movement. She would not engage in any dialogue, and I was not close enough to grab her. I radioed Communications to contact the fire department because I was sure she was going to jump. I have dealt with jumpers before, but I had never seen someone so committed to the act.

I was totally focused on her and was trying to figure a way over the barrier without her jumping when the other sergeant quietly rolled up and passed behind me on foot. Her attention was divided between working up the courage to jump and me. It was quite obvious that she did not want me to try to stop her. It gave the other sergeant the opportunity to get over the barrier without her noticing. I think that at that point she decided she could not jump headfirst and turned around. She was now on the outside of the west railing of the bridge with her toes on a small protrusion on the outside of the rail, her back to the river. The other sergeant tried to speak to her. She murmured for him to stop. He pretended he could not hear her and asked her to speak up as he closed the distance. This allowed me to get over the barrier.

She let her toes slip off the edge. She was hanging by her fingertips.

We both moved in and grabbed her wrists. Once we got hold of her, we pulled her over the rail and put her down onto the sidewalk. She was sobbing, and her body was shaking with emotion. I handcuffed her because I didn't want her to break free from us and jump over the bridge. I asked her name, but all she did was cry. Two constables came up, and we turned the woman over to them. They took her to the hospital. It turned out she wasn't a woman but a girl, seventeen years old.

I looked at the other sergeant and thanked God he'd been there. I got back in my patrol car shaking with adrenaline and told him in an animated voice how close that was. He was calm, eerily so. We had known each other for several years by this point, and I was puzzled by his lack of emotion. I told him I was going back to the office and possibly never going back out again. I drove back to the station to leave my report. As I pulled up in the back lot, the other sergeant came speeding in and pulled up beside my car. With all the energy I had expected on the bridge, he exclaimed how very close that was. I think it took a couple minutes for the intensity of what we had just been through to sink in.

Because incidents like this are not criminal matters, you do not really get follow-up on the people you deal with. There are privacy issues, and the local health district has to do the follow-up. All you can do at the end of the day is hope for the best.

The other sergeant went on vacation to Mexico at the end of his night shift. The very next night, I told our story to our shift on parade as I was turning them out for our last night. I told them how the other sergeant had used a tactic to close the distance and allow us to grab the girl. When the sergeant told the girl to speak up because he could not hear her, human nature and common decency made her look at him long enough for me to get over the barrier.

Several hours later, there was a jumper on the Victoria Bridge. The senior constable used the same tactic, and she and another constable saved a sixteen-year-old youth. Later in the night, she came in and excitedly told me that the story I had told on parade made all the difference in how they responded.

20.

Cold Saves

Almost every night, in all seasons, police get calls about intoxicated people who are passed out outside. The Saskatoon Police Service weathered a furious storm and all sorts of allegations involving intoxicated people in the winter. The allegations are public knowledge. What is not public knowledge is the number of people who are saved by police officers every day and every night.

I have no idea how many intoxicated people I have dealt with in my career. It's easily in the thousands, people whose state of intoxication so robbed them of their ability to care for themselves that they would fall wherever their bodies failed them. Passing out in the grass in a vacant lot or city park in warm weather does not have the dire consequences of passing out somewhere unseen when the temperature is −20, −30, and −40.

Sometimes when I would arrest intoxicated people in extreme weather conditions, I would be angry with them. I failed to see how powerful their addictions were, and how those addictions had come to impair their judgment. Freezing to death has nothing to do with race. Poor reasoning and decision-making skills are not restricted to any one race. Nor is the reckless disregard for one's personal safety restricted to the young.

The thin line between arresting intoxicated people and filling a detoxification unit—the drunk tank—and investigating deaths by misadventure hinges on alert citizens and diligent patrol officers. I've seen many instances where citizens will call in about intoxicated persons inadequately dressed out in the severe cold. Officers will respond and locate the individuals and, depending on how cold or intoxicated they are, the officers will call an ambulance or cart them off to jail until they are sober enough to care for themselves.

On other occasions, officers will spot an intoxicated person and decide to arrest them for their own safety. To me, every one of these incidents—and there are a lot of them—is a save.

Dealing with drunken people is the least glamorous aspect of patrol work. It is thankless and can be challenging. Some drunken people are pleasant and co-operative, but some are not. They will swear at you, or call you a racist no matter what their race is. Sometimes they will try to assault you. Sometimes they will vomit or urinate in your car. You want to tell them that you are just trying to save them from freezing to death, but most of the time they don't care.

I told the people I worked with to treat intoxicated people calls as emergencies if the weather is extreme. Depending on a person's state of intoxication, fifteen or twenty minutes could make the difference between crippling injuries or death and spending the night in the drunk tank. It's hard not to be judgmental of people who have placed themselves in danger. I think it is a measure of a person's character when they perform their duty even when their duty is repetitive and thankless.

Around the time the Saskatoon Police Service was being investigated by the RCMP, my partner and I took a call about a person in an isolated area on the railway tracks. It was late at night, −30, with high wind chill. The area was barely visible from the road. A person had called in because they had heard someone yelling, and the call was dispatched as an unknown problem. We went to the area of the call and got out of our patrol car. There were no tracks in the snow in the area the caller had indicated. But sounds have a way of carrying when it's extremely cold; even with the wind, we heard some muffled yelling.

We trudged through the ditch up onto the railway tracks. In the distance, we saw tracks going up the bank on the opposite side of where we were. As we walked down the tracks, we could hear a man yelling and swearing. He was in the ditch. We went to his location. He was freezing and drunk. He was heavyset and very belligerent. You could see by his tracks that he had crossed an area behind a granary into a field and seemed to be trying to go to some apartments a half a kilometre to the west. In his drunken state, he crossed over a field and went through some trees before losing steam in the deep snow of the ditch.

If it weren't for the person who had called in the unknown problem, I am sure this man would have died. Instead, he was arrested and transported to cells. All the way, he called my partner and me racist pigs and accused us of dropping people off outside of town. At first we were angry, railing against all the people criticizing our police service, and wishing some of them could see what we were doing on that night. The reality, though, was that we were doing our job the way we were supposed to. The reality of it is that these types of incidents will always be a part of the job, and the responsibility of all police officers to do the work is something they can never walk away from, whatever the criticisms.

I love the people who make the calls to us about drunken people. Even if they don't stay to see what happens, at least they have made the call. Whenever a citizen has called about a drunken person because they believed that person was in danger and I make an arrest, I like to call the complainant back and thank them for possibly saving the arrested person's life.

Policing in the winter can present daunting challenges to officers. Extreme temperatures and high wind-chills are hard on equipment and people. The natural tendency is to stay in your patrol car as much as possible.

I like it when it's extremely frigid, except when I'm working. I often tell people that it makes a lot of us a lot smarter. Extreme cold can make most people operate more efficiently. Unfortunately, there are those who don't, and it has caused much heartache and cost for us all. A lot of people do not adjust their driving habits for extreme winter conditions. Traffic accidents are for the most part preventable; people just need to slow down and think, put time in perspective, and drive to arrive. A police officer has a higher chance of being struck, injured, or killed by other drivers at a traffic accident, especially in the winter, than they do of being shot.

Functioning in the cold is as much about attitude as it is about being properly equipped. The Saskatoon Police Service is still a bit behind when it comes to properly equipping patrol officers with adequate winter gear. It's difficult to find a balance between presenting a quality public image and being dressed warmly enough to function in bitter conditions. Boots and trousers are two areas where patrol officers are inadequately provided for. Uniformly provided windproof pants and felt-lined boots would allow officers to safely work for long periods of time in extreme conditions. Twenty-seven years in, we still improvise. K-9 officers, Public Order unit members, and some Traffic members have the proper equipment, but the vast majority of Patrol members are left to their own devices and will sometimes have to violate policy to keep warm.

Marked patrol cars all have in-car computers and cameras and have to be left running for extended periods of time so that the systems continue to function. This is a constant source of complaints from the public.

Patrol officers are out there day after day, night after night. Most of us do not give them much thought when we are home in the comfort of our living rooms and the warmth of our beds. I do, and always have. I grew up in Northern Ontario, and I know how extreme cold can test your resolve and your ability to be diligent.

A couple of years later, I was with another partner and again it was an extremely cold night. There were not many calls, and just about everybody wanted to stay inside. The bars had closed, and we were just patrolling alleys when we saw a pair of legs sticking out from behind a Loraas disposal bin. We got out to investigate and saw a male dressed in a jean jacket passed out cold. At first I thought he was dead. It turned out he was just drunk. He was a big guy and woke up combative, and we had to handcuff him. We took him to jail. He recognized me, and all the way in the arrested male cursed and swore about how I only arrested my own people and how I worked for the white man.

Experience has taught me that for the most part, you can't reason with drunken people. They are going to do what they are going to do regardless. The bottom line is, a save is a save, and if you think of it in those terms, this kind of police work is pretty good stuff.

21.

A Family's Shame

I was going through years of my police notebooks, and it struck me how many times over the years I had dealt with the same people. There is a lesson there: never do the victory dance when you arrest somebody. Quite simply, no matter what the offence, the offender will eventually get out of jail and be back in your city again.

Your post-arrest behaviour will set the tone for your relationship with your arrests for years to come. If you're fair but firm with your arrests and let them know you're just doing your job, they will remember that. This is one of those hard-learned lessons I started to realize fairly early in my career. I would arrest people and they would get a federal penitentiary sentence, but within a relatively short period of time, they were back. Very few offenders serve their full time. Parole and statutory release allow offenders to be released back into the community, sometimes with years of their sentence unserved.

The vast majority of people who commit a criminal act are people who are in a bad place at the time. Some addicts actually beat their addictions. When they have turned their life around, how do you want them to remember you? As a vindictive and judgmental officer? Or as a fair and decent police officer who did his job without bias or sarcastic commentary?

Some criminals are so hateful, no amount of empathy or compassion will make a difference to how they feel about you. You will know when you're dealing with one of those people. Still, if you are professional in all your dealings with criminals, you will have the advantage provided by the high ground.

As a police officer, you have to be aware that everything you do is in the public eye. Everything you do and say is subject to scrutiny. Fair enough, given the authority society has given you.

Everyone has an opinion about the police. Some people can go through their whole life without ever having talked to a police officer, and still they would have an opinion. This is why it is important to teach young police officers the weight of their words and deeds.

I have been called a hardass many times in my career. I've made thousands of arrests. People make up their own minds about who you are. There are a lot of people who, for whatever reason, hate me for what I do and have done. The one thing they do not realize or consider is that I get it. I understand how much of what I have done has affected their lives. I understand how much pain the arrest of a loved one has caused people. I also understand how much pain the crimes committed by the people I have arrested cost the victims. I know no one person is truly alone, without love or family. Sometimes I just get an overwhelming feeling of sadness at the tragedy and wish that the events that brought me into their lives had never happened. But they did, and I was there.

Something always happens at the end of a shift.

I was on day shift when a call came in. There had been a stabbing at a hospital. I was only a couple blocks away and arrived quickly. As I went into the hospital, I was directed by security and staff to the fifth floor. You try to take in as much information as you can as you're approaching a scene, but it was clear there was bedlam. Nurses and doctors were running, looks of horror and disbelief on their faces. I did not know if I was passing a suspect or suspects as I moved through the halls. Basically, I knew nothing.

When I got to the fifth floor, I was met by a security officer who handed me a manila envelope containing a bloody buck knife. The security officer was a bright, well-spoken kid who would have been a good police officer. He directed me to a room where another security officer was standing at the door. I passed by a four-patient room where doctors were working on the victim. It did not sound or look promising. The room was sprayed with blood, and all the machines' alarms were sounding.

Passing the security guard at the door, I found a native grandmother who apparently did not speak a lot of English, and a native man who appeared to be about forty years old. He was a big man, heavyset, with droopy eyes. He wore a hospital gown and was covered in blood. The grandmother wore heavy clothing, as most people from the north tend to do. She wore a kerchief in the same style I remembered women wearing when I was a child. She had two long, traditional braids framing her face.

The young officer told me that the male had stabbed a man in his room, and the grandmother had taken the knife afterwards. They were leaving the hospital when the security officer intercepted them on the ground floor as they were coming out of the elevator.

I placed them both under arrest, the male for attempted murder and the grandmother for being a party to attempted murder. I handcuffed them both. I felt bad handcuffing the grandmother, but I did not know if she had any other weapons and I did not want to search her. She clearly did not understand her rights and spoke in Cree to the male, who turned out to be her son. The male, who was flushed with bloodlust and very agitated, replied "uh huh" in a deep voice when I asked if he understood his rights.

It was eerie. I could hear people yelling and frantically attempting to save the victim. I had just finished arresting the male when a doctor came in the room and told us very matter-of-factly that the victim was dead.

It took a while for other units to get there because it was shift change. I re-arrested both the grandmother and her son for murder. The grandmother just looked at me and in a quiet voice and broken English asked for me to call her daughter, indicating that her daughter would make everything right. The male just grunted yes.

From what I knew so far, this crime was almost incomprehensible. The hospital is supposed to be a place of caring and healing. The bloody crime scene I briefly saw was like a gaping wound when set against the sterility of the hospital.

The suspect began to tell me that the deceased male was putting magic on him. I knew nothing of the victim at the time, other than the fact that he was dead.

I notified our Communications section that the victim had died and requested Major Crimes and Identification section to attend. As other officers I began to arrive, I requested them to secure the scene and start taking witness statements. I asked one officer to transport the grandmother in and advised him he needed a Cree interpreter. A patrol sergeant arrived, and I quickly briefed him and then escorted the male to my patrol car. As we walked through the hallways, I could feel people staring. Grief, shock, and disbelief were pliable emotions from everyone we passed.

I transported the man to the Saskatoon City Police detention area.

He was glassy-eyed, still filled with adrenaline, and I felt still very dangerous. The suspect spoke in grunts. He knew what he had done. He knew the man was dead.

The suspect's hands, arms, and hospital gown were covered in blood, so he had to stay handcuffed until a forensics officer swabbed the blood off. He was angry because I did not unhandcuff him. I had to sit in an interview room with him for quite a while, waiting for the investigators.

It was a tense and trying couple of hours before I was relieved. The suspect was in a place I knew nothing of and had just stabbed a man to death. I was not really traditional when it came to those parts of my native heritage which dealt with evil spirits and magic. The weight the suspect and his mother placed on these beliefs was beyond my understanding. This man obviously had mental health problems, and because of his mental state I did not want to take advantage of him until he spoke with a lawyer. He did not seem to care.

As it turned out, the male, a native man from northern Saskatchewan, was at the hospital for treatment of diabetic issues. He was placed in a four-patient room. He was an angry and difficult patient. The suspect believed the victim was using magic against him, so he called his mother and asked her to bring him a knife for the coming struggle. His mother, a traditional and elderly woman, believed what her son told her and brought him a knife. When the moment was right, my suspect set upon the victim, a man in his seventies, stabbing him numerous times, killing him. While the murder was occurring, a paralyzed man in the next bed watched in horror and disbelief, not knowing if he was next.

The local media covered the story. At a press conference, the defence lawyer railed against the police for the arrest of the grandmother. He called the arrest ludicrous. The crown prosecutor at the press conference announced that the charge against her had been stayed. I had never received a call from the crown prosecutor telling me that the arrest was unjustified, nor was there any other explanation as to why the defence lawyer was allowed to ridicule police actions—in this case, my work. At this point my career, however, I was pretty thick-skinned and did not see any reason to pick a fight. It would not have changed the outcome.

The arrested man was found not to be criminally responsible and was sent to an institution. The victim's family made no comment to the media, and I never did receive any feedback from the homicide detectives who had investigated the crime after I left the hospital, just one callous remark about how easy the crime scene was to process.

A couple of years later, I was loading my car at the start of a night shift and I saw the murderer by himself on a park bench just outside of the station. He was mumbling and probably fighting a new set of demons. I assume he was living in a group home somewhere in the downtown area because I've seen him many times since, shuffling about mumbling, in place I still know nothing about.

I use him as a teaching point now. When I see him, I will grab a constable and ask what they think. Most say that he obviously has mental health problems but that he looks harmless enough. Then I tell them this story.

I often tell people when I arrest them that their arrest isn't the end of the world. It's just something they will have to deal with, and how they deal with it will make all the difference when it's over.

Sometimes the offence was so egregious that there was a feeling of grim satisfaction at getting the offender. But it never makes you feel any less sad.

I understand the frustration of watching a loved one be handcuffed and sent to jail. I understand the hate. I understand the love so hard to part with. I did my job relentlessly, but I got it. A mother's tears, a father's pain, and a family's shame when someone is arrested—none of it happens in a vacuum.

I left a mark which will endure or fade away, depending on the people I have affected, for better or for worse. That is just the way it is.

Soon to be condos, this low-rent building was often home to addicts and petty criminals, and a good training ground to test new recruits. (PH-SM-8, courtesy Saskatoon Public Library – Local History Room)

22.

The Truest of Warrior Spirits

I don't remember what year it was. I was at home watching a television show called "William Shatner's 911." I don't remember the episode, but I think it was some sort of medical emergency. My heart began to pound and I became anxious. My wife told me to relax, it was only a television show. I had to get up and get out of the room. Something in the show triggered a memory, which triggered a physical reaction. What we both did not know at the time was that that episode of anxiety was the opening salvo in my battle with post-traumatic stress, a battle almost all first responders will have to fight at one time or another in their career.

In all my years of police work, I have no idea how many dead people I have seen. As to be expected, I have seen all manner of death. Murders, suicides, accidents, and natural deaths all have to be attended to by the police. It is not only the deaths that can eventually weigh upon your mind. Raw violence, violent injuries, and survivors' grief get a billing as well.

One of the saddest things I have dealt with over the years is finding people, young or elderly, who have died totally alone. They were only found when a neighbour called in because they hadn't been seen for a while, or worse yet when a smell was coming from a residence. You force your way in, never knowing why a person would choose to shut themselves off from the world to die alone, without anyone to care. How can someone's despair and mental illness be so utterly complete?

During the first few years of police work, you want to be the tough guy for your coworkers and your family, so you don't talk a lot about the things you see and do. Eventually, you start to talk about things, but it's often cloaked in black humour, or you tell the story for the story's sake.

What I have learned, and learned the hard way, is that it is good to talk over things you have seen and done, with people of like mind and people in general. Every time you do, you release a little bit of the pressure that inevitably builds up inside you.

I let mine build and build over the years.

Every time I had an episode of anxiety, I would blame it on the adrenaline dump after a serious call. When you go to a serious call, your body charges you full of adrenaline. In a stressful situation, your body pumps the blood from your extremities to your core, preparing for fight or flight. Your heart rate jumps. When the situation is done, however, your body struggles to resume normal function.

If I had an episode of anxiety when I was off duty and far removed from a call or incident, I would blame it on too much caffeine or fatigue. So build and build it did, until the fatal pursuit in 1999. Up until then, every dead person, every tragedy, and every horrible thing I had seen or done I had mentally stuffed into a room to be dealt with later. After the pursuit, my later had arrived. It was like I was in a long hallway and every door to every room I had stuffed a trauma into opened up at the same time.

Still I tried to deny it. I still wanted to be the tough guy, but it did not always work. At work, I kept working; there was always enough to keep me busy and distracted. It was when I was off duty and at night when the demons made their moves. I would have bouts of anxiety at the weirdest times, usually when I least expected them. Anything could trigger the feeling: a song, a movie, or just watching people go about their lives. An unexpected loud noise could start my heart pounding and dry the saliva in my mouth.

Eventually, I saw it for what it was. It was my body's way of dealing with all the horrible things I had seen over the years. None of this is new to most people nowadays. Post-traumatic stress is well documented, and its existence in first responders is pretty much accepted, but it is and will always be the most personal of battles. It can rule you and make you ineffective, or you can work your way through it.

I made just about every mistake you can make trying to deal with the effects of seeing and doing things most people will likely never have to experience. Initially, I started with outright denial. I thought I was too tough. When I would clear a violent incident or death, other officers would ask me if I was all right, and I would almost always answer,

"Yeah, why wouldn't I be?" I overcompensated with my family and tried to protect them from any calamity. In doing so, I restricted their growth and independence of thought. I tried to control the things I thought I could control, and when I could not, I would get frustrated and irritable. I moved on to alcohol, and that didn't really help either.

So now my career is over. Am I symptom free? Honestly, the answer is no. Nor, realistically, will I ever be. Some things scar you for life, and there's not a thing you can do about it.

I use perspective as an ointment. The proper perspective can help minimize traumas to manageable proportions. The most recent example of putting things in perspective is when I think of the horror the officers, paramedics, and firefighters must have felt when they responded to the shooting of the schoolchildren at Sandy Hook Elementary School in Newtown, Connecticut. I've seen dead children before, but one at a time. By God's mercy, I have never had to see a classroom full of children who had been shot. Even if they never took another call for the rest of their careers, those first responders saw and did enough on that one day to give them nightmares for the rest of their lives.

Now as a sergeant, I tell my people what I have learned so that they will not have to repeat the same journey I have been on. Even then, all you're doing is just giving them a little more insight because you cannot shield everyone from everything, and how they deal with trauma is as individual as they are.

When something serious or traumatic occurs, I encourage them to talk about it, to tell the story as many times as they need to. I emphasize that the trauma and its effects are cumulative, and if they don't deal with the way they feel at the time, it will just compound the stress they will inevitably feel later in their careers. I watch them constantly for the signs. Overcompensation, nervousness, and weight loss are common. The inability to concentrate, loss of interest in things at work, and irritability are red flags. Sometimes, those are just part of everyday life and not symptoms of post-traumatic stress, but you still have to check. I tell my story of the long hallway and hope that they will never have to walk down one of their own.

While saying all of this, I chose to be a police officer, and I chose to be on the street for almost my entire career. It was a certainty that I would see tragedy and that it could not be helped. I accepted the inevitable. I just did not expect to see as much.

Everybody has a breaking point. Sometimes it was obvious, and officers accepted it and moved on to other jobs within the police service where they did not have to be the first one at a call. There is no shame in saying you have had enough.

It took me years to realize that some officers were leaving Patrol for reasons other than the better hours. Sometimes I could just be clueless, or as I have been told by a few people, for a smart guy I could sometimes be a dumb ass. I was fiercely loyal to Patrol and to the officers who manned the front lines. I would be contemptuous of officers who wanted to leave. Some officers genuinely wanted to go on to investigations so they could have time to investigate things in detail and challenge themselves in a different way. Others bravely acknowledged that they had had enough of the speed and violence of Patrol. Maturity has given me enough insight to realize that they were not jumping ship.

When I first started with the Saskatoon Police Service, post-traumatic stress was called burnout. It wasn't acknowledged. The police culture was such that admitting something bothered you was virtually unheard of. Everyone had to be a tough guy, and the few women had to be even tougher. It's possible that some of the people I clashed with over the years were suffering the effects of post-traumatic stress and never knew what it was. I will give them that as a possible explanation for some of the things that happened.

I think most police organizations have acknowledged the stress that comes from the job and have taken steps to help officers right after a critical incident occurs. Police officers are expensive to train, and the cumulative experiences they have had are hard to recreate for new officers, so their mental well-being is a common-sense investment. I know the Saskatoon Police Service has taken great strides in this area since 1999.

Inevitably, there are a few officers who take advantage of the rest of us by claiming stress and going off work because they can. Those officers actually add to my stress. To me, it is unconscionable that any officer would book stress leave if they were not truly stressed. It waters down the seriousness of stress-related issues. They should be ashamed. There are so many officers over the years who could have legitimately booked stress leave and did not. The ones who take advantage of the system are beneath contempt and dishonour the brave officers.

If you think the police you see in the movies or on television—the ones who shoot, chase, and fight for the entire shift and then go for beers—are real, however, you are in for a long and hard ride if you actually become a police officer. Prior knowledge and acknowledgment of post-traumatic stress is the best defence you can give yourself and your officers. Still, there is a certain amount of schizophrenia when it comes to stress and acknowledging its effects. Everybody wants to be brave and show they can take whatever comes at them. It is human nature, and it is part of the culture of all first responders, police, paramedics, and firefighters. Even late in my career, when I dealt with something that shocked or horrified me, and when asked if I was okay, I would almost inevitably answer, "Yes, me I am a tough guy from Ontario Nord!" But unless you are the truest of warrior spirits and can move from one horror to another, year after year, you will eventually have to deal with what you have seen or done.

My partner and I were leaving the station and beginning a night shift. Some directives and orders had been issued and we were discussing what we thought was the stupidity of them. Generally, we were just bitching about the job. We came to a red light. A man who looked about thirty and was stricken with some disease that caused him to be crippled was crossing the street in front of us. He struggled with every step, and it took him several cycles of the lights to get across. Still, as he passed in front of our car, he took the time to smile at us. My partner turned and looked at me and said, "Ernie, we really don't have any problems." I couldn't have agreed with him more.

Perspective is a wonderful thing. It can take down barriers when you think you are up against the wall. It can lighten your load when you feel the burden is crushing you.

I really never was a desk guy. (Courtesy Saskatoon Police Service)

23.

24/7—The Regular Stuff

For years, I never really considered the complexities of the whole operation of the Saskatoon Police Service. I was always at the sharp end: patrol. I either took other sections for granted or considered them soft cops. For years, I referred to the administration contemptuously as "those people." For years, I referred to anybody who was not in the front line as "tourists."

As you get older, you become a bit more laid back. I realize everyone has a different role, and human nature makes everyone feel that their role is the most important one. There are certainly some jobs within the service I would never have considered, but those positions were created by a need, and somebody had to step up to do the job.

My goal was to stay on the street for my entire career, and I almost did it, but every once in a while I got stuck inside by default.

Saskatoon Police Service Patrol Division works two twelve-hour days and rotates to two twelve-hour nights. There are four platoons providing twenty-four-hour coverage, 365 days a year. Each platoon has, on average, thirty-five patrol constables and two K-9 constables. They are supervised by three patrol sergeants and four inside sergeants. The inside sergeants run the Communications section, the detention area, and readers' positions. The readers' positions are to ensure quality reports are submitted before they are presented to the Crown. They also forward and monitor requests for the Crown Prosecutor's Office and monitor investigations. The communication sergeant supervises up to eight special constables, who take calls and dispatch officers from the communications centre. The detention sergeant has two special constables and oversees every prisoner and transaction that occurs in the detention area. He also releases prisoners who can be released.

Augmenting the platoons are four Community Resource officers. In the summer, these officers ride bikes, and in the winter, they walk the beat. They are supervised by a sergeant who covers two platoons, so you get him for two days out of the four. Depending on the day of the week, you can also have a Weekend Support team of up to eight constables and a sergeant to reinforce the presence on the street. There are two Weekend Support teams. The second weekend team—again eight constables and a sergeant—is dedicated to special projects. In the mix, the Traffic section assigns up to four constables to perform traffic enforcement within the platoon rotation.

In theory, it sounds like a staff sergeant (or as they are commonly referred to, a watch commander) has a lot of people to supervise. The reality of it is that on the average day, you can have up to twelve officers off duty from the platoon's thirty-five-officer strength. As watch commander, you have no say over the time off allowed for weekend support teams or traffic officers. Specialty patrol units like the Community Response unit and Weekend Support work different hours and are off earlier than the regular patrol constables on night shifts. Once you factor in members who are sick, injured, or on training courses, the on-the-street strength of a platoon watching over 250,000 people is not all that impressive.

That said, before you start barricading your house and hiring private security, you have to realize that policing is an expensive business. I was only talking about uniformed police, the ones who come when called. Supporting the uniformed officers are a host of investigative sections, the plainclothes officers who monitor high-risk offenders and police the street gangs. There are school resource officers. There are community liaison officers. There are school officers. The Saskatoon Police Service has integrated sections where plainclothes investigators work with the RCMP. The Drug section, Criminal Intelligence and Internet Child Exploitation units are all integrated. Commercial Crimes, like fraud, has a section, and Property Crimes, like stolen autos and break-and-enters, are separate units. There is a Major Crimes section to investigate murders and unexplained deaths. There is a Sex Crimes unit and a Personal Violence unit. In case we miss anything, there is a General Investigations section.

There are some units that draw their members from all of these other units, including Patrol when they need to, like the Emergency Response team, the Explosive Disposal team, and the Crisis Negotiation team.

In behind these people is an administration, officers who job it is to plan training and research equipment. Technical officers are tasked with and specialize in retrieving electronic data from in-car camera and audio systems. They analyze seized computers and cell phones. There are the executive officers who plan the future and analyze the present. They do the budgeting and buy the gas and bullets.

February 4, 2013, was one of those days I was inside. The regular staff sergeant was on holidays. Over the past few years, as a senior patrol sergeant, I would cover the staff sergeant's position when he was on holidays or courses. I found myself as acting staff sergeant about three months of the year. When I first started doing the job, I would do the bare minimum of the paperwork and go out on the street and make arrests like I was still a constable. One summer night, a call came in of an assault in progress in the 300 block of Avenue G South. I rolled up, the first officer at the scene, and a male came running out to the street covered in blood, followed by a male holding a bottle by the neck. I drew my gun and proned him out on the ground. Other officers began to arrive, and we quickly established that the assault had taken place inside the house. Several people had run into the house when I first rolled up on the call. We went in after them and ended up arresting three more people.

While I was doing this, my cell phone kept on ringing. When I finally got the opportunity to answer, it was the media. Viewers were sending video from their cell phones of us at the call. All media inquiries were directed to the cell phone the watch commander carried, and they wanted to know what was going on. It took this and several more incidents like it over the next few years for me to realize that when I was in charge, sometimes I had to stay out of the fight and be available to lead.

I have attended thousands of dispatched calls over the years. Every call had to come in over the phones at the Saskatoon Police communications centre. A special constable had to get the information, usually from an excited, sometimes frantic caller who may have never called the police before, and then format it into a call. The call-taker had to sort through the information and try to give the responding officers a picture of what was happening. The call-taker relayed the call to the dispatcher, who in turn dispatched the call, all on a computer-aided dispatch system. They are surrounded by screens and phones, and the two dispatchers man the radios.

The call-takers and all the communications staff do not disconnect from the call, especially if it is a dangerous or tragic call. They listen, knowing that they have just sent officers into chaos, and wait while the incident unfolds. They hear calls for back up. They hear the stress and anguish. They hear all of it, and call all the people who need to be called: ambulances, firefighters, detectives, and whoever else can help the officers who are at the call. As it all unfolds, unless they have done something wrong, we take them for granted. They go home at the end of the day not always knowing if the people they have sent to a call are all right, what happened to the victim, or how everything turned out. In an incredibly difficult job, stress is an understatement.

Over one hundred thousand reports are left every year by the Saskatoon police. There are nearly two hundred thousand dispatched calls. Not all dispatched calls result in a report, and not all calls result in a dispatch. On average, thirty special constables spread over four shifts and supervised by four sergeants handle this incredible amount of information.

When a wife-beater or a murderer or any other criminal is put in jail, officers leave their reports. They dictate them into a phone and then off they go to the next calamity or to their home. The report sits in a pending job queue and is typed by priority. A report where a person is in custody is the highest priority. A civilian clerk types the report. I had not always thought of the impact our words have on these clerks. The graphic descriptions of injuries and traumas must at some level weigh on their minds. We ask a lot of people and sometimes take them for granted.

Not until I was an acting staff sergeant did I get an appreciation for the tremendous of amount of behind-the-scenes work these clerks do. How much they do, translated into numbers, is daunting. On average, four hundred police officers leave 100,000 reports a year, not counting investigation reports, tickets, and miscellaneous entries. The ones who do the lion's share of the work are the ones who work with the shifts in the same rotation as the platoons. The Saskatoon Police Service Patrol division works twelve-hour shifts, two twelve-hour days and two twelve-hour nights.

On top of everything else those clerks do, they enter warrants and track cases and convictions. Four supervisors for four shifts oversee this massive undertaking. Every story, every horrible incident is typed and organized into a report to be scrutinized by the many people in the many systems for many years to come. How could you not admire and appreciate this much work?

If you can make it with the Saskatoon Police Service as a special constable in the Communications section or as a civilian clerical staff member, you can make it anywhere.

I always resisted working inside the station. But Monday was a day shift, and there were generally enough administrative duties to occupy the entire day whether I liked it or not. It was our platoon's second day shift. I woke up at 3:30 a.m. I drove to Tim Horton's, got a coffee, drove to work, showered, and put on my uniform. Even though I knew I would probably be inside all day, I wore my gun belt and body armour. I didn't want to get used to not wearing all of my equipment. I went to the office—yes, the office—and relieved the night watch commander at about 4:30 a.m. He said it had been quiet night.

I booked onto the computer and picked ZZ Top's first greatest hits CD as the background music for the mind-numbing task of reading new directives and e-mails. Between 4:30 and 5:30, I assigned missing persons cases, and sorted court notices and mail. At about 5:30, a call came in that there was a fire in a building complex under construction at the intersection of Diefenbaker and Centennial Drives. The intersection was a major chokepoint in the morning commute. I knew this would cause big problems for those fighting the fire. Some constables from the night shift were at the scene, but I had not yet received an update from them. I radioed them and asked if a sergeant was at the scene, but the night shift's sergeants were in the station switching off with our sergeants. The day-shift patrol sergeant for the division where the fire was immediately grabbed his gear and headed out to the fire a full half-hour before he was due to start.

I then went up to the parade room. The parade room, which doubles as a classroom, is just like you see on television. Officers go there prior to the start of the shift to answer roll call and be briefed on who is wanted or any other relevant information. I called roll call and spoke about safe winter driving because we had lost so many patrol cars to accidents in the month of January. It was a simple message really: "Drive to arrive." Just prior to parade, officers came to me and told me that a lot of patrol cars were out of service because of camera and computer trouble. I had to go to the quartermaster and authorize him to issue the keys to officers whether the computer or cameras were working are not. On parade, I told the officers we were police officers long before we were cameramen or computer operators.

Right after the six o'clock parade, the patrol sergeant at the fire asked for four patrol cars to control traffic at the fire. He had also called the City of Saskatoon to provide barricades. I did a quick media release advising that traffic was restricted in the area of the fire. I signed some overtime sheets for night shift guys who had arrested an impaired driver close to the end of their shift. It was more paperwork. Then I turned out the seven o'clock shift. I gave them the same message: do not wreck any cars and to be careful on the street. As I watched them file out of the station, I wished I were going with them. Instead, it was more paper-and-file assignment. The sergeant at the fire kept me regularly updated. At about 8:30, the firefighters were done except for the post-fire investigation. The traffic restrictions were lifted, and the patrol sergeants came in for their morning meetings with their respective division inspectors.

Meetings have always been one of my Achilles' heels when it comes to getting along with administrators. I have always believed that if it is important enough, the meeting will occur as a necessity. Setting meetings at scheduled times with no urgent agenda just seemed to be a poor method of exercising leadership. I learned over the years that one of the easiest ways to erode morale and cohesiveness is to give people tasks that are not meaningful. Setting meetings to talk about things you already know and threatening discipline if people do not attend does not endear you to people.

While the three patrol sergeants were in their meetings, a call came in from a care home. The staff there were holding down an emotionally disturbed man who was wielding a knife and refusing to drop it. Several patrol units volunteered for the call, which was on the east side of the city. One of the officers who was en route asked if any of the less-than-lethal weapons carried by emergency response team members while they are on regular patrol—Tasers or shotgun rounds containing beanbags —were available in case the situation got out of control. The sergeant who had been at the fire and the East patrol sergeant ran out of their meetings and went to the call. If they had been on the street instead of in a meeting at the station, their arrival time would have been much better. As it was, officers were able to safely disarm the suspect before the patrol sergeants arrived. It was not even 9 a.m. yet.

I had to go to my own meeting at 9:30, and once I was done there, it was back to paperwork. In the watch commander's position, you are also required to issue equipment, field calls from other police services, and take public complaints. Pretty much everything and every question people do not know the answer to gets directed to the watch commander's office.

Two of my patrol sergeants were constables acting in their roles. One of the acting sergeants had a lot of experience in the acting role and had fulfilled every other patrol sergeant's position at one time or another over the past four years. The other acting sergeant had just come back to Patrol from a plainclothes position. She had been at a sudden death the day before and I wanted to ask her if she had any concerns or questions. She told me it was routine until a Hells Angels member who was related to the deceased woman showed up started yelling and making a difficult situation worse. She talked him down until he was civil and finished the call.

One of the officers who was at the call of the knife-wielding emotionally disturbed man came in and briefed me on what had transpired at the call. He also added that the recruit he was training had done well and had engaged the suspect without any hesitation. It was good news. I always wonder how recruits will do at their first violent calls. Several more officers dropped in to discuss files and investigations they were conducting, and I had not even noticed that we were into the afternoon.

Just before 2 p.m., a call came in of an armed robbery at a business in the 1200 block of Idlywyld Drive. It was everything I could do not to jump into patrol car and head out to the scene. I listened to the radio as a suspect was spotted. He ran from the acting sergeant who had been at sudden death the day before. Trapped in the office, I could only listen while numerous units made their way to where the suspect was last seen. K-9 units deployed, and within a moment or two, the suspect was found hiding in a garden shed. The money and the knife he had used were recovered. I telephoned our public relations officer and let her know. There had been an armed robbery the day before at a hotel, and the suspect matched the description. I called the staff sergeant in charge of the General Investigation section to tell him, and he sent two detectives to interview the suspect when he got into detention.

I went up to the detention area to get a look at the arrest in case I ever got back on the street again. When I got there, he was collapsed on the floor and, in my opinion and based on my experience, faking a seizure. Still, we were required to call an ambulance. The paramedics who showed up were a brother and sister. Their mother was a detective sergeant. It turned out the arrested male was faking, and he remained in police custody. While all of this was going on, there was a constable in detention processing an impaired driver. I had not even heard that call. I was so proud of all the work my officers were doing that day.

The sergeant who had been at the fire had transported the armed robbery suspect into detention so that the constables could finish their investigations. I don't think he expected the arrest to fake a seizure or to be tied up as long as he was. While he was in the office doing his paperwork, a call was received indicating that a federal prisoner who was serving time for manslaughter had escaped a couple weeks ago was at an address in central Saskatoon. The troops went there and stopped a vehicle leaving the address. They confirmed with occupants of the vehicle that the escapee was in the house. They convinced him to surrender, and he was taken into custody without incident.

By this time, it was time to do the payroll. My day in the office was almost over. I went home after congratulating all my guys on the great work they had done on what was a good day.

Though I knew I could do it, in my heart I was never an inside cop. I also know that those men and woman can do their job without me, and it kind of makes me sad—in a good way. They do not need me. They've got it covered. Enough said.

About the Author

Born in 1961 in a remote Northern Ontario community and a member of the Missanabie Cree Band raised off reserve, Ernie Louttit attended a one-room school until grade eight. He was boarded out in another town for high school, which led to him quitting in grade eleven to work for the Canadian National Railway. At seventeen, he joined the Canadian Forces, serving with the Princess Patricia's Canadian Light Infantry and military police.

In 1987, he was hired by the Saskatoon Police Service as only the third native officer in the force's history. He has spent his entire twenty-six-year career on the streets of Saskatoon's west side, an area until recently beset by poverty and terrible social conditions. Louttit served during the most tumultuous years of the Saskatoon Police Service, always in the front lines as he learned to navigate the difficult issues of crime, race, and community expectations – both white and native. He became known on the streets as "Indian Ernie," to him a badge of honour. He officially retired as a sergeant as of October 29, 2013. He continues to reside in Saskatoon and is married with four grown children. This is Ernie's first book.